MEDITERRANEAN
DIET COOKBOOK
FOR BEGINNERS

A **STEP-BY-STEP** PRACTICAL GUIDE TO PREPARE
DELICIOUS & HEALTHY **MEDITERRANEAN RECIPES**.

DIANA GRECO

TABLE OF CONTENT

4.   INTRODUCTION

6.   MAIN INGREDIENTS

7.   FAQ

9.   CONVERSION TABLES

MEDITERRANEAN RECIPES

12.   FIRST DISHES

50.   SECONDS AND SIDE DISHES

84.   DESSERTS

108.   APPETIZERS AND BRUNCH

134.   MEAL PLAN

The Mediterranean Diet represents an eating pattern typical of countries bathed by the Mediterranean Sea.

This type of approach to nutrition is recommended by International Scientific Societies in the context of prevention of the most common diseases.

When we talk about the Mediterranean diet, we do not refer to a vegetarian diet, although foods of plant origin have an important relevance in this type of diet.

Likewise, it does not refer to a bread and pasta diet or a "nutrient-poor" diet.

The Mediterranean Diet is a wholesome diet, and the foods that comprise it assume a functional role. It is not a fattening or slimming diet; it refers to particular qualitative aspects of food, not its energy content.

The traditional Mediterranean Diet is not just a way of eating, but a set of social habits and cultural traditions, handed down by populations.

Therefore, we are not talking about a restrictive regimen, but a true way of life.

There is no single Mediterranean Diet, but we can identify a common pattern that has these characteristics:

- Abundance of plant-based foods (vegetables, fresh fruits, vegetables, nuts, legumes, bread and pasta and other grains such as spelt, barley and oats);
- Use of olive oil as the main source of fat;
- Prevalent consumption of seasonal foods;
- Fish, eggs, white meat consumed in moderation;
- Daily but moderate consumption of dairy products;
- Low consumption of red meat;
- Regular use of herbs that allow flavoring of foods without overdoing salt or fatty seasonings;
- Moderate intake of wine with meals;

Reduced consumption of sweets, which are best eaten only at feasts.

In the Mediterranean Diet, the amount of food to be consumed during meals is defined in several ways, the most commonly used being the food pyramid.

One of the most representative food pyramids is the American food pyramid, developed by Walter Willett, M.D. of the Harvard School of Public Health.

Willett's pyramid recommends:

- Consume daily unrefined grain derivatives, vegetables, legumes, fruits, nuts, olive oil, cheese and yogurt;
- Eat red meat monthly;
- Eat fish, eggs, white meat, sweets weekly;
- Moderate red wine with meals;
- Abundant water;
- Daily physical activity.

This pyramid was revised in 2003 by two influential American epidemiologists from Harvard, Walter Willett himself and Meir Stampfer.

These presented a new proposal with some significant differences.

In the new pyramid, fats do not all have the same nutritional value, and carbohydrates were divided into simple and complex.

In the previous pyramid, all fats were placed toward the top (meaning you should consume them in moderation), but in the new pyramid, vegetable fats have been placed at the bottom, which suggests consuming them every day.

Alcohol in moderation

MONTHLY
Red Meat, Sweets, Sugary Drinks

WEEKLY
White Meat, Fish, Eggs

DAILY
Vegetables, Fruit Legumes, Milk Cheese

DAILY
Bread, Cereal Pasta, Olive Oil, Potatoes, Rice

Daily Exercise, Weight Control

OLIVE OIL

This represents the centerpiece of the Mediterranean Diet and determines its flavor. It is certainly the most widely used fat because of its very high oleic acid content (70-86%), which helps keep cholesterol down.

It is rich in polyphenols and has antioxidant characteristics that protect us from cancer.

Olive oil is not only important for its properties, but also because it is a good substitute for fats such as butter or lard.

WHOLE GRAINS

These are at the base of the food pyramid, along with vegetables and fruits. When we talk about whole grains we refer to foods such as corn, barley, rice, wheat, and spelt.

Several researches state that grains have a beneficial effect on health. Foods composed of whole grains, substantially reduce the risk of cardiovascular disease, diabetes and cancer, as well as also play a crucial role in body weight management and digestive health.

A recent analysis of 25 studies, confirmed that intake of 3 servings per day of grains correlated with a reduced risk of colorectal cancer.

FRESH FRUITS AND VEGETABLES

Fruits and vegetables are low-calorie foods that are rich in fiber, water, vitamins and minerals.

Fruits and the fiber they contain, increase the sense of satiety and consequently leads to not overconsuming other types of foods.

Vegetables should be consumed at every meal, while fruits would be recommended to be consumed away from meals, perhaps as a snack.

It is important to always choose seasonal fruits and vegetables to limit the intake of harmful substances used in agriculture.

FISH

It is an excellent source of protein, vitamin D, polyunsaturated fatty acids and mineral salts such as selenium, phosphorus and potassium. Special attention should be paid to the presence of Omega-3 fatty acids that protect our cardiovascular system, decreasing the risk of coronary heart disease, atherosclerosis, thrombosis and hypertension.

LEGUMES

Often referred to as "poor man's meat," they are instead an exceptional food, both for the presence of protein and slow-absorbing carbohydrates.

Legumes also contain a good amount of minerals, vitamins and dietary fiber, which promotes satiety.

WINE

What makes it perfect is the presence of antioxidants such as quercetin and esveratrol, which have the power to protect proteins, lipids, and nucleic acids from free radical attack.

It is clear that it is not possible to eliminate free radicals with wine, because this would involve excessive alcohol consumption. However, the concept remains valid that a good glass of red wine, can help reduce the risk of cardiovascular disease while improving lipid status, blood pressure, insulin sensitivity, and HDL cholesterol levels.

It is crucial to emphasize that in a Mediterranean Diet all meals of the day, starting with breakfast, must be balanced and contain all the nutrients we need.

Always pay attention to the quantities and especially the balance of nutrients.

In a classic Mediterranean diet, 55-60% of energy should come from carbohydrates, 12-15% from protein and 25-30% from fat.

DOES THE MEDITERRANEAN DIET MAKE YOU LOSE WEIGHT?

Be wary of those who sell you the Mediterranean Diet as a slimming diet. They are lying to you.

The real Mediterranean Diet, as I explained to you earlier, is not a diet for losing weight or gaining weight, but represents a real way of life.

Of course, losing weight is possible and it is also simple if you know how to do it.

All you have to do is incorporate within your diet a calorie deficit.

To achieve this, you only need a few simple steps to follow:

1. Calculate your daily caloric needs.
2. From your requirements subtract 20%.
   Example: if your daily caloric requirement is 1,500Kcal, subtract from that a 20%. 1,500 - 20% = 1,200Kcal.
3. Monitor your meals to make sure you meet your daily 1,200 Kcal.

DIET FLEXIBILITY AND WEIGHT LOSS

Weight loss is a slow and, above all, steady path. Far better to lose a little weight each month than to lose a lot of weight quickly, only to regain it all back with interest.

To be sure that your diet will be a success, it is important to indulge in a few rewards now and then, but always in moderation.

Within this book there are recipes that you can choose for your daily diet, and there are others, more caloric, that would be better to choose on holidays.

The truth is this: if you are not in an obesity situation, then you can relax and eat almost anything you want, but in moderate quantities.

It is clear that a lasagna is not a particularly dietary dish, however, nothing prohibits you from eating a small piece without overdoing it.

In some desserts you will find butter. Can you eat it? Of course you can, just don't do it daily and in excessive amounts.

CALORIE GUIDE TO RECIPES

I have seen that there are many cookbooks that enter the relative calories under each recipe.

This is possible if the recipe is extremely simple and by its nature portioned.

Example: 5 oz of Greek Yogurt + 1 oz of whole grain cereal.

In this case determining calories would be simple, but do you really mean to tell me that you needed a cookbook explaining how to mix yogurt with cereal?

The recipes you'll find in this book are slightly more complex than a slice of bread with cherry tomatoes, so indicating the calorie intake of each recipe would have been virtually impossible.

If counting calories is very important to you because you want to follow the Mediterranean Diet to lose weight, then what I recommend you do is get an app on your smartphone that allows you to enter all the foods that make up the recipe.

You will then have to weigh everything to do as accurate a job as possible.

My advice, in case your weight problem is not considerable, is simply not to overdo it.

On the other hand, if your physical condition is worrisome or you are obese, see a doctor and avoid getting your way. Health is not a game.

GUIDE TO INGREDIENTS USED IN RECIPES

In the recipes I offer in this cookbook you may find foods that, for one reason or another, you won't be able to find around. Don't worry! Substitute them!

If you can't find a particular type of mushroom, replace it with a mushroom of another type. Same thing with regard to fish!

If you can't find a particular cheese such as Pecorino Romano, use classic Parmesan or a similar cheese.

In short, don't let a little bump in the road stop you. Making a few changes to recipes is certainly not the end of the world; in fact, it could be a great way to discover even new flavors!

VOLUME EQUIVALENTS (DRY)

US STANDARD	METRIC (APPROXIMATE)
1/8 Teaspoon	0.5 ml
1/4 Teaspoon	1 ml
1/2 Teaspoon	2 ml
3/4 Teaspoon	4 ml
1 Teaspoon	5 ml
1 Tablespoon	15 ml
1/4 Cup	59 ml
1/2 Cup	118 ml
3/4 Cup	177 ml
1 Cup	235 ml
2 Cups	475 ml
3 Cups	700 ml
4 Cups	1 l

WEIGHT EQUIVALENTS

US STANDARD	METRIC (APPROXIMATE)
1 Ounce	28 g
2 Ounces	57 g
5 Ounces	142 g
10 Ounces	284 g
15 Ounces	425 g
16 Ounces (1 Pound)	455g
1.5 Pounds	680 g
2 Pounds	907 g

TEMPERATURES EQUIVALENTS

FAHRENHEIT (F)	CELSIUS (C) (APPROXIMATE)
225 °F	107 °C
250 °F	120 °C
275 °F	135 °C
300 °F	150 °C
325 °F	160 °C
350 °F	180 °C
375 °F	190 °C
400 °F	205 °C
425 °F	220 °C
450 °F	235 °C
475 °F	245 °C
500 °F	260 °C

VOLUME EQUIVALENTS (LIQUID)

US STANDARD	US STANDARD (OUNCES)	METRIC (APPROXIMATE)
2 Tablespoons	1 fl.oz.	30 ml
1/4 Cup	2 fl.oz.	60 ml
1/2 Cup	4 fl.oz.	120 ml
1 Cup	8 fl.oz.	240 ml
1 1/2 Cups	12 fl.oz.	355 ml
2 Cups or 1 Pint	16 fl.oz.	475 ml
4 Cups or 1 Quart	32 fl.oz.	1 l
1 Gallon	128 fl.oz.	4 l

FIRST DISHES

Ragù Napoletano
Neapolitan Ragout

Servings: 4 people

Ingredients

- 21 oz beef, cut into pieces
- 32 oz tomato sauce
- 1 tbsp tomato paste
- 2.8 cups water
- 1 onion
- 2 carrots
- 1 celery stalk
- 1 garlic clove
- Basil
- 3 tbsp olive oil
- Salt and pepper to taste
- ½ cup red wine
- 12.5 oz penne rigate type pasta

DIRECTIONS:

1. Peel the carrots, onion and garlic, and clean the celery stalk well. Cut these 4 ingredients into very small pieces.
2. Pour the olive oil into a high-sided pan. When hot, add the chopped vegetables for the "soffritto". Fry for at least 3 or 4 minutes. Turn them often so they don't burn.
3. In the meantime, take the pieces of beef, add salt and pepper, and rub the meat. When the sauté is ready, place the pieces of meat in the pan and brown first on one side and then on the other. Then pour in the red wine and let it evaporate well.
4. Once the wine has faded, add the tomato puree, tomato paste, water, basil leaves, and salt. Mix everything well and cook on a low flame for at least 3–4 hours.
5. Cook separately, in salted water, the pasta you prefer. I advise you to always use a "ribbed" type of pasta so that the sauce sticks to the pasta. Drain the pasta al dente and pour it back into the cooking pot. Season first with a generous ladle of sauce and stir, then serve and pour another ladle of sauce for each portion.
6. The meat, which will be very tender, can be enjoyed as a second course accompanied by a pan-fried vegetable.

TIPS:

My grandmother used to make the meat sauce the day before we had to eat it.
In Naples, the ragù is prepared on Saturday evening after dinner and is cooked for a couple of hours. On Sunday morning the fire is turned back on and it is cooked for another 3–4 hours. In this way, the sauce becomes even more concentrated and sticks to the pasta even better.
If you are going to prepare the ragù according to this tradition, be very careful to always keep the flame low and not burn the sauce. If this is drying out too quickly, add more water.

Genovese
Genovese

Servings: 4 people

Ingredients

- 19 oz rump (veal) tip in pieces
- 53 oz golden or white onions
- 3 carrots
- ½ cup red wine
- 3 tbsp olive oil
- Salt and pepper to taste
- 13 oz short pasta, such as penne, ziti, rigatoni
- Parmesan cheese to taste

DIRECTIONS:

1. Rub the meat with 1 tablespoon of olive oil, salt, pepper and set aside.
2. Peel the onions and cut them in half and then into slices not too thin.
3. Pour the remaining 2 tbsp olive oil and the carrot, previously peeled and chopped into small pieces, into a high-sided pan and sauté. Place the meat in the pan when the oil is hot and brown it well on all sides. Then pour in the red wine and allow the wine to dry completely.
4. Add the onions. Salt, stir and turn the heat down to low. Cover the pot with a lid, leaving a small air gap, and let it cook for at least 3 hours, stirring occasionally. If the mixture dries out too much, it risks burning, so add a glass of water and continue cooking. At the end of cooking the onions should be totally wilted.
5. Cook the pasta separately in salted water, draining it al dente. Once the pasta has been drained, pour it directly into the pot with the Genovese and stir everything gently, keeping the pot on a low flame.
6. Once served, add a sprinkling of Parmesan cheese.

TIPS:

In my house, we used to make a single dish, so the pasta was also served with the meat in the same dish.
If you prefer to use the meat as the main course, before pouring the pasta into the Genovese sauce, remove the pieces of meat and some of the sauce to keep it moist.

Pasta e Patate
Pasta and Potatoes

Servings: 4 people

Ingredients

- 28 oz potatoes
- 1 onion
- 2 carrots
- 2 tbsp olive oil
- 1 sprig thyme
- Salt and pepper to taste
- 12.5 oz mixed pasta or ditalini or broken spaghetti
- Parmesan cheese to taste

DIRECTIONS:

1. Rinse the potatoes, remove the skin and dice them all about the same size.
2. Peel the onion and carrots and cut them into very small pieces.
3. Place a high-sided pot on the stove and pour the olive oil inside. When the oil is hot, add the onion and carrot. Let it sauté for a couple of minutes and add the potatoes, salt, pepper, and the sprig of thyme. Mix well and sauté for a couple of minutes.
4. Then pour in enough water to completely cover the potatoes, lower the heat and cook until the potatoes are soft.
5. When the potatoes are ready, lower the pasta into the same pot and consider whether more water is needed to prevent the pasta from sticking. In the end, the dish should not be brothy but creamy, so adjust while the pasta is cooking by adding a little water at a time. Taste and check if you need to add more salt and once the pasta is cooked, serve.
6. Sprinkle the portions with a little parmesan cheese and enjoy!

TIPS:

A debate has arisen in Italy over the traditional recipe for "pasta e patate", whether or not to use provolone cheese. The real traditional recipe is without provolone cheese; however, I can assure you that if you add some diced provolone cheese when the pasta is almost cooked, you'll be licking your lips from the taste. Try the two versions and choose your favorite.

Ragù alla Bolognese
Bolognese Ragout

Servings: 6 people

Ingredients

- 21 oz ground beef (not too lean)
- 9 oz ground pork (not too lean)
- 3 cups tomato puree
- 2.5 cups water
- 1 white onion
- 2.4 oz celery
- 3 carrots
- 3 tbsp extra virgin olive oil
- ½ cup red wine (white is also fine)
- 0.2 cup whole milk
- 1 sprig fresh rosemary
- Salt and pepper to taste

DIRECTIONS:

1. Peel the carrots and onion and wash the celery stalk well; cut the vegetables into very small pieces.
2. Take a pot with high sides, put it on the stove, and pour the 3 tbsp of olive oil. As soon as the oil is hot, add the chopped vegetables and fry for at least 2 minutes.
3. In the meantime, clean and finely chop the rosemary, add it to the sauté and cook for another 2 minutes, stirring occasionally.
4. Once the sauté is ready, add the ground beef and pork and, using a fork, separate the meat to cook evenly. Add salt and pepper. As soon as all the liquid from the meat has been absorbed, add the wine and let it evaporate completely, always over high heat (the wine must always evaporate completely before adding the sauce because otherwise, it could leave an acrid taste to the final dish).
5. As soon as the alcohol has evaporated, add the tomato puree, water and another pinch of salt. Stir well and move the pot over a small fire. Cook for at least 3 hours over low heat, covering the pan with a lid. Stir the sauce from time to time and make sure it is not drying out too quickly.
6. At the end of cooking add the milk and mix everything together.

TIPS:

This sauce is perfect for dressing pasta, but in my family, we often used it to make lasagna. In this case, I remember that my grandmother did not add milk to the sauce but, when she prepared the lasagna pan, for each layer, she added the béchamel sauce and mozzarella cheese into small pieces, while on the last layer she sprinkled a generous handful of parmesan cheese.

Pasta e Fagioli
Pasta and Beans

Servings: 4 people

Ingredients

- 7.4 oz mixed pasta or ditalini or broken spaghetti
- 10.5 oz boiled borlotti or cannellini beans (either ready canned or dried to be soaked and boiled are fine)
- 6 oz fresh red tomatoes (peeled tomatoes are fine)
- 2 garlic cloves
- 3 tbsp extra virgin olive oil
- Fresh parsley
- Salt and pepper to taste

DIRECTIONS:

1. If you choose dried beans, you'll need to cook them before you start preparing the pasta and beans. Place them in a tall, large bowl, cover with plenty of water and 1 tsp of baking soda. Stir and let them sit for at least 6–7 hours. I usually do this process before going to bed at night. After 6–7 hours rinse well with water, transfer them to a pot with high sides and cover them totally with water. Cook over medium heat for about 1 hour. They will be ready when they are soft, then taste. If you have a pressure cooker, this process will take much less time. Just pour the dried beans into the pot, cover them with water, close the pot well and put it on the stove. When the pot starts to whistle you will have to lower the flame and cook for another 20 minutes and the beans will be ready.
2. Now let's move on to the preparation of the traditional Neapolitan pasta and beans. Peel the garlic cloves and crush them lightly.
3. Pour the olive oil into a high-sided pan and bring it to heat. Once the oil is hot, brown the garlic well.
4. In the meantime, rinse and dry the cherry tomatoes well, cut them in half and put them in the pot. Add the finely chopped parsley and cook for about 7–8 minutes.
5. Add the beans (they must be well drained from the cooking or canning water), salt and pepper and mix everything together. Fry for 10 minutes and cover with water.
6. As soon as the water starts to boil, wait about 15 minutes and drop the pasta into the same pot. Consider that the final mixture should not be brothy but creamy so do not overdo the water and at most add it slowly if you need it during the cooking of the pasta.
7. Taste the pasta and assess whether it needs more salt. When the pasta is cooked through, turn off the heat and let it rest in the pot for about 2–3 minutes before serving.

TIPS:

My grandmother loved to add another ingredient.
When she brought the dishes to the table, she would cut some onion into very small pieces and let it fall raw onto her plate of pasta and beans. I have to say that even today, years later, I do it too because besides reminding me of beautiful moments of my childhood, the taste is really good!

Frittata di Spaghetti
Spaghetti Omelette

Servings: 4 people

Ingredients

- 14 oz spaghetti
- 4 eggs
- 5 oz parmesan cheese
- Sunflower or peanut oil
- Salt and pepper to taste

DIRECTIONS:

1. Bring salted water to a boil and lower the spaghetti. Once cooked, drain them al dente otherwise you risk breaking them later. Let them cool for about 20–30 minutes.
2. In a large bowl, pour the eggs, Parmesan cheese, 2 pinches of salt and pepper and mix well with a hand whisk. Once the mixture is creamy, pour the spaghetti into the bowl and, with the help of two forks, mix everything well so that the spaghetti is completely amalgamated with the egg mixture.
3. In the meantime, take a pan at least 11 inches in diameter, place it on the stove and pour in the seed oil. The oil should cover the pan for at least 0.04 inches in height. When the oil is hot pour the spaghetti mixture inside and let it cook for about 15 minutes; as soon as the base is golden brown, flip the omelette.
4. Help yourself to a large enough lid: Place the lid on the pan and use one hand to hold the lid firmly in place, while using the other hand to turn the pan upside down. Do this process away from the stove. Once the frittata is on the lid you can gently transfer it to the pan to cook the other side until golden brown and crispy.
5. Once the omelette is ready, leave it to rest on a few sheets of absorbent paper. You can eat it warm or cold, it will be a real treat.

TIPS:

My dad loved spaghetti frittata, he would take it with him to work as a snack at least 2 times a week and my grandmother would cook one so big that he would share it with all the guys who worked in the same restaurant as her.
He, however, preferred it with a slight variation, namely "red".
When my grandmother would make spaghetti, she would dress it with a fresh tomato sauce quickly prepared and then continue with the classic preparation I explained above.
Also, try this variation which is even tastier.

Spaghetti Aglio, Olio e Peperoncino
Spaghetti With Garlic, Oil and Chili Pepper

Servings: 4 people

Ingredients

- 14 oz spaghetti
- 4 tbsp extra virgin olive oil
- 1 large clove of garlic
- Chili to taste
- Parsley to taste
- Salt to taste

DIRECTIONS:

1. Prepare the pot with salted water where you will cook the spaghetti.
2. While the water comes to a temperature, prepare the rest. Peel the garlic and remove the soul (the soul of the garlic is that central thread that you find once the garlic is divided into 2 parts), then cut it into small pieces.
3. The chili should be washed, dried well, and cut into small pieces, adjust according to your taste for quantities.
4. Rinse the parsley, dry it well and chop it finely.
5. Take a frying pan large enough to hold the spaghetti and pour in the olive oil. Heat the oil and add the garlic, taking care that it does not burn, otherwise the dish will taste bitter. Then add the chili pepper, cook for a minute and then turn off the heat.
6. Lower the pasta when the water boils and drain when it is very al dente, keeping a ladle of the cooking water to one side.
7. Turn the heat back on under the pan and pour in the spaghetti, the ladle of cooking water, and the parsley, and stir until the water is absorbed.
8. Serve the spaghetti piping hot and enjoy the taste of this quick and easy dish!

TIPS:

You can enrich this dish by sprinkling it with crumbled taralli or toasted breadcrumbs. Simply take a frying pan and make it very hot, crumble the bread crumbs into very small pieces and toast it for a few minutes being careful not to burn it. Finally, add the crumbled taralli or toasted bread crumbs directly onto the spaghetti.

Pasta al Forno
Baked Pasta

Servings: 4 people

Ingredients

- 12 oz rigatoni type pasta
- 8 oz mozzarella
- 4 eggs
- 3.5 oz salami
- 1 onion
- 2 carrots
- 4 tbsp olive oil
- 24 oz tomato puree
- 1.5 cups water
- Salt to taste
- A few basil leaves
- 3.5 oz parmesan cheese

DIRECTIONS:

1. Start by preparing the sauce: peel and chop the onion and carrots into small pieces.
2. Take a high-sided pot and pour in the olive oil, onions and carrot. Turn on the heat and cook, stirring occasionally, for at least 2 minutes.
3. Then pour in the tomato puree, basil and water, add salt and cook over medium heat for about 1 ½ hour.
4. Meanwhile, prepare 4 hard-boiled eggs; in a small saucepan pour enough water to cover the 4 eggs and bring to a boil. As soon as the water boils, add the eggs and set a timer for 9 minutes. When the timer expires, drain the eggs, rinse them under cold water and let them cool.
5. Meanwhile, cut the mozzarella and salami into small pieces.
6. When the eggs have cooled, peel and chop them into small pieces.
7. Now prepare the pasta. Put a large pot of salted water on the stove and when it comes to a boil, lower the pasta. Be careful, the pasta must be drained very al dente so that after cooking in the oven it will not be too soft.
8. Drain the pasta and put it back in its pot without water. Add 2–3 ladles of the sauce to the pasta and stir.
9. Take a high-sided baking pan and cover the bottom with some sauce, then a few ladles of pasta, and cover everything with mozzarella, salami and eggs. Then again a couple of ladles of sauce and repeat the process until you have finished the ingredients. On the last layer add the parmesan cheese.
10. Place the pasta pan in a ventilated oven preheated to 350°F and bake for 30 minutes. Once that's up, take the baked pasta pan out of the oven and wait 10 minutes before serving. Enjoy!

TIPS:

Baked pasta is a very versatile dish. If you don't prefer salami, you can replace it with cooked ham and if you prefer provolone to mozzarella, it's still okay.

My grandmother often prepared it using Bolognese sauce as a base, she didn't use eggs and salami and only added mozzarella cheese before baking.

Spaghetti con le Vongole
Spaghetti With Clams

Servings: 4 people

Ingredients

- 14 oz spaghetti
- 28 oz clams with shell
- 2 tbsp olive oil
- 1 garlic clove
- Parsley to taste
- Salt to taste

DIRECTIONS:

1. Take a large pot for cooking spaghetti, fill it with water, add salt and put it on the stove, and bring it to a boil.
2. In the meantime, rinse the clams and let them drain in a colander.
3. Peel the garlic clove, rinse the parsley and chop it finely.
4. Get a skillet large enough to hold the clams and spaghetti. Pour in the oil and place it over medium-high heat. When the oil is hot, add the garlic clove and fry for a few minutes without burning it.
5. Add the clams and cook until all the clams have opened. Turn off the heat.
6. Drop the spaghetti when the water boils and, when they are very al dente, move them with a fork directly into the clam pan (turn the heat back on) and add 2 ladles of the cooking water. Stir until the water is almost completely absorbed.
7. Add the parsley, turn off the heat and stir. Eventually, you should create a little cream around the spaghetti.
8. Serve the spaghetti still hot.

TIPS:

If you prefer you can also shell the clams once cooked, leaving only a few with the shell to decorate the dish at the end. The procedure remains the same, nothing changes.
I absolutely advise in favor of preparing this dish using fresh clams and not frozen or frozen shelled clams, you will lose so much flavor. Rely on a fishmonger that sells fresh shellfish.

Risotto con Zucca
Pumpkin Risotto

Servings: 4 people

Ingredients

- 11 oz Carnaroli rice
- 21 oz pumpkin
- 1 onion
- 0,4 gallons vegetable stock
- 2.8 oz parmesan cheese
- ½ glass white wine
- 1.7 oz butter
- Salt and pepper to taste
- 2 tbsp olive oil

DIRECTIONS:

1. To prepare the vegetable stock the procedure is as follows: fill a high-sided pot with water and add salt, a peeled and halved onion, a peeled and halved carrot, 2 tbsp of tomato puree and a celery stalk. Cover with a lid and cook for an hour or so on medium flame. Once ready, strain the broth, remove the vegetables and keep warm.
2. Now let's move on to the preparation of the risotto.
3. Remove the skin and seeds from the pumpkin, cut it first into slices and then into cubes.
4. Peel the onion and cut it into very small pieces. Take a frying pan and pour in the olive oil, once heated add the onion and fry it for about 2 minutes, stirring occasionally to prevent it from burning and sticking.
5. Now add the pumpkin and salt. Brown the pumpkin for about 3–4 minutes over low heat, stirring so that it does not stick; now add a ladleful of hot stock and cook the pumpkin for about 15–20 minutes until it is soft and creamy. Add more broth if it dries out too quickly.
6. Put a large frying pan on the stove, once hot drop the rice and let it toast for about 2–3 minutes, stirring often so it doesn't stick.
7. Deglaze with white wine and wait for it to dry.
8. Once ready, transfer the rice to the pan with the pumpkin and stir. Add a ladle of broth and stir. Each time the broth dries up add more broth until the rice is cooked.
9. Taste and add salt and pepper to taste. Turn off the heat, add the butter and Parmesan cheese and stir gently to cream the risotto. If you prefer a creamier risotto, add a little more stock while stirring.
10. Let the risotto rest for 30 seconds before serving.

TIPS:

Once the risotto is served, you can add a sprinkling of thyme which will give a great aroma and flavor to the dish.

Spaghetti Cacio e Pepe
Spaghetti With Cheese and Pepper

Servings: 4 people

Ingredients

- 12 oz spaghetti
- 7 oz pecorino Romano medium seasoning to grate
- 0,1 oz black pepper in grains
- Keep the spaghetti cooking water aside

DIRECTIONS:

1. Put on the stove a pot with other edges with salted water and bring to a boil; as soon as the water boils, lower the spaghetti.
2. Finely chop the black peppercorns, pour them into a non-stick pan and toast over low heat for a couple of minutes being careful not to burn them. Add a ladle of cooking water and cook the pepper again.
3. As soon as the pasta is al dente (I suggest you cook it 2–3 minutes less than the cooking time indicated on the package) move it with a fork into the pepper pan, add a ladle of cooking water and continue to do so until the pasta is cooked. Add the cooking water only when the water previously poured in has been absorbed.
4. In a bowl grate the Pecorino cheese and add a ladleful of the cooking water, mix vigorously with a whisk until a creamy mixture is created. If the cream is too hard, add more cooking water (the cream should still be thick but not lumpy).
5. As soon as the pasta is fully cooked add the pecorino cream and gently toss the spaghetti. The end result should be spaghetti covered in a creamy layer.
6. Serve and add a sprinkling of pecorino cheese and a pinch of pepper, enjoy!

TIPS:

This dish is very simple and inexpensive but will surprise you with its taste. Be very careful when preparing the pecorino cream and in general when you add cooking water to the ingredients, I recommend you always add it little by little to avoid overcooking and making the pasta too liquid.

Spaghetti all'Amatriciana
Spaghetti all'Amatriciana

Servings: 4 people

Ingredients

- 12 oz spaghetti
- 14 oz peeled tomatoes
- 1 oz pillow
- 2,6 oz pecorino romano (pdo, to grate)
- 0.3 cup white wine
- 1 tbsp extra virgin olive oil
- salt to taste
- 1 fresh chili pepper

DIRECTIONS:

1. Take a high-sided pot and bring the water for cooking the pasta to a boil. Add salt as well.
2. Take the pillow, remove the rind and cut it into slices about 0.2 inches thick;
3. Take a frying pan, put it on the stove, and let it heat up. Add the pillow and brown it on a low flame for 7–8 minutes. The fat of the pillow should become transparent and the meat crispy. Stir often being careful not to burn it.
4. When the fat has melted, pour in the white wine, turn up the flame and let the alcohol evaporate. Transfer the strips of guanciale to a plate and set them aside.
5. Grate the Pecorino Romano and keep it aside.
6. In the same pan where you cooked the pillow, add the whole, seeded chili pepper and the peeled tomatoes that you have roughly crushed by hand. Cook the sauce over moderate heat for about 10 minutes and add salt to taste.
7. When the water for the pasta has come to a boil, lower the spaghetti and cook them al dente.
8. Remove the chili from the sauce, add the strips of the pillow and stir to mix.
9. Drain the spaghetti and pour it into the pan with the sauce. Very quickly toss the pasta to mix well with the sauce and add 1 tbsp of oil while stirring.
10. Serve and sprinkle with grated pecorino Romano cheese.

TIPS:

Amatriciana is quite a spicy dish, adjust the amount of chili pepper according to your taste and be careful to remove all the seeds from the chili pepper before using it.

Pasta alla Gricia
Pasta alla Gricia

Servings: 4 people

Ingredients

- 12 oz rigatoni
- 9 oz guanciale (already peppered)
- 2 oz pecorino Romano cheese to grate
- Salt and black pepper

DIRECTIONS:

1. First, prepare the guanciale: remove the rind, cut it into slices 0.2 inches thick and cut into strips.
2. Put a high-sided pot on the stove and add water and salt to cook the pasta. Bring to a boil.
3. In a very hot pan, brown the guanciale over medium-high heat for about 10 minutes, stirring often to avoid burning it. When lightly browned, set aside, leaving the cooking liquid in the pan.
4. In the meantime the water for the pasta will have come to a boil, so cook the rigatoni for 2–3 minutes less than the time indicated on the package.
5. Grate the pecorino finely and keep it aside.
6. Pour a ladleful of the cooking water into the still hot pan of guanciale and stir to create an emulsion.
7. Drain the rigatoni al dente and add them to the pan (which will be on the stove with a medium-high flame) and finish cooking by tossing and stirring often, so that the starch released from the pasta mixes with the fat of the sauce.
8. When the pasta is fully cooked, remove the pan from the heat and add the grated Pecorino. Dilute with a little cooking water (2–3 tbsp) and stir until creamy. Add the browned guanciale and stir again.
9. Serve immediately and sprinkle with a pinch of ground pepper. Enjoy your meal!

TIPS:

It is said that the recipe for Gricia was invented by the shepherds of Lazio who, with the few ingredients available, prepared a dish as simple as substantial. A Gricia made to perfection must be creamy and tasty with just the help of cheese and cooking water: in our family, we have always used rigatoni pasta to make this tasty sauce, but a different type of pasta such as spaghetti will also be perfect.

Spaghetti alla Nerano
Spaghetti Nerano Style

Servings: 4 people

Ingredients

- 12 oz spaghetti
- 24 oz zucchini
- 7 oz provolone del Monaco
- 2 cloves garlic
- Extra virgin olive oil (both for seasoning and frying)
- Basil
- Salt and pepper

DIRECTIONS:

1. First, wash and dry the zucchini and cut them into thin rounds.
2. Take a frying pan and pour plenty of olive oil; when the oil is hot, fry the zucchini for about 2 minutes. Make sure the oil is hot and not cold and turn the zucchini halfway through cooking. The zucchini should be golden brown. Once golden brown, move them to a sheet of paper towels and add salt.
3. Grate the provolone and set it aside.
4. Take a high-sided pasta pot, fill it with water and add a handful of salt and some pepper.
5. In a separate pan add 2 tbsp of oil and the peeled and crushed garlic cloves, sauté for 1 minute, then add the fried zucchini and a handful of basil, and let everything cook together over a gentle flame for about 2 minutes.
6. In the meantime, cook the spaghetti for half the time indicated on the package and drain, keeping the pasta cooking water to one side. Pour the spaghetti into the pan with the zucchini, adding 1 ladle of cooking water from the pasta.
7. Continue cooking the pasta over medium heat until the noodles are al dente and creamy.
8. When cooked, turn off the heat, stir for 15–20 seconds and then add the grated provolone cheese and toss away from the stove, adding 1 tbsp of the cooking water if you notice the spaghetti is too dry. They should come out creamy and blended.
9. Plate and taste!

TIPS:

My grandmother loved this dish and once it was served, she decorated it with 2 mint leaves, the flavor and the fresh scent created a delicious contrast.
You try it too!

Spaghetti alla Puttanesca
Spaghetti alla Puttanesca

Servings: 4 people

Ingredients

- 12 oz spaghetti
- 28 oz peeled tomatoes
- 1 oz anchovies in oil
- 0,3 oz capers in salt
- 1 sprig of parsley
- 3.5 oz Gaeta pitted black olives
- 3 garlic cloves
- 2 small dried chilies
- 3 tbsp extra virgin olive oil
- Salt to taste

DIRECTIONS:

1. First rinse the capers under running water to remove excess salt, then dry them and chop coarsely with a knife.
2. Take the pitted olives and crush them with the blade of a knife.
3. Wash, dry, and chop the parsley.
4. Put a high-sided pot filled with salted water on the stove to bring to a boil to cook the pasta.
5. In a large pan pour the oil, the whole peeled garlic cloves, the chopped dried chili and the anchovies. Add the capers. Fry everything over medium heat for 5 minutes, stirring often so that the anchovies will melt and release all the flavors. At this point pour in the peeled tomatoes lightly crushed with a fork, stir with a spoon and cook for another 10 minutes over medium heat.
6. Meanwhile, cook the spaghetti al dente.
7. When the sauce is ready, remove the garlic cloves and add the crushed olives. Sprinkle the sauce with chopped fresh parsley.
8. When the pasta is al dente, drain it and bring it to the pan, tossing it for ½ minute, just enough time for all the flavors to blend.
9. Plate the spaghetti and serve piping hot.

TIPS:

Given the presence of capers and anchovies, spaghetti puttanesca is a very savory dish. Be careful with the salt to avoid making them overly salty.

Pesto alla Genovese
Pesto Genovese

Servings: 4 people

Ingredients

- 2.4 oz basil
- 2,4 oz extra virgin olive oil
- 1.8 oz parmesan cheese (aged at least 30 months)
- 1 oz pecorino cheese
- 1 oz pine nuts
- 2 garlic cloves
- 0,1 oz coarse salt

DIRECTIONS:

1. To make pesto alla Genovese, first, remove the leaves from the basil sprigs and place them in a colander. Rinse them briefly under cold running water, then dry them well by patting and rubbing gently.
2. Take a mortar, a marble one would be ideal and put the peeled garlic cloves inside, remove the soul and cut in half. Work the garlic with the wooden pestle until you obtain a cream.
3. At this point add the pine nuts and continue to pound. When you have crushed them, add the basil leaves and coarse salt. Always start with percussion movements first and then continue with rotating movements. Collect with the help of a spoon the ingredients from the inner edges of the mortar to obtain a uniform pesto.
4. When the consistency is creamy and smooth, add the pecorino in chunks and pound in the same way to incorporate it, then add the Parmigiano Reggiano and do the same thing.
5. When all the ingredients have been reduced to a cream, pour in the oil and pound for a few more moments.
6. The pesto alla Genovese is ready to be used to dress pasta or toast.

TIPS:

Pesto alla Genovese can be used immediately or kept in the refrigerator, in a jar well covered with oil, for up to 4 days. Alternatively, you can freeze the pesto in small jars.
To obtain a perfect pesto you must use good quality basil: if the basil is not of good quality it will tend to oxidize and turn black.

Fettuccine Alfredo
Fettuccine Alfredo

Servings: 4 people

Ingredients

- 14 oz flour
- Remilled durum wheat semolina for dusting to taste
- 4 medium eggs
- 2.8 oz butter
- 2.8 oz parmesan cheese Pdo grated
- Salt and pepper to taste

DIRECTIONS:

1. First, prepare the fresh egg pasta: sift the flour in a bowl (leave some aside) and add the eggs. Work the mixture with your hands until you get a homogeneous dough, then transfer it to a work surface and finish kneading; if the dough seems too soft you can add some flour, if it is dry you can add a little water. When the dough is smooth and elastic, form a ball, wrap it in plastic wrap and let it rest at room temperature for 30 minutes so that the gluten relaxes and the dough is easier to roll out.

2. After half an hour, lightly dust the work surface with flour and divide the dough into 4 parts: knead one part at a time and leave the remaining dough covered with plastic wrap to prevent it from drying out. Lightly flour the part of the dough that you are going to roll out with a rolling pin and pass it through the pasta machine, starting from the widest thickness; add a pinch of flour to prevent the dough from breaking.

3. Repeat the operation several times until you reach the desired thickness. If you don't have a pasta machine, you can roll out the dough with a rolling pin, rolling it out several times until it is thin.

4. At this point, divide the sheets into 2 or 3 parts, depending on their length, and pass them through the machine again on the penultimate number to prevent them from shrinking.

5. Dust the sheets with semolina and let them dry for a couple of minutes.

6. In the meantime, boil a large pot of salted water that we will use to cook the fettuccine.

7. Once the dough has dried, take a sheet of dough and roll it up on itself from the shorter side, taking care not to press it down so that the overlapping layers don't stick together. When you have obtained a cylinder of regular shape, cut into rounds of about 0.15–0.16 inches thick with a knife with a smooth blade.

8. Unroll the rondelle grabbing them by one end and roll the fettuccine obtained around your hand to form a sort of nest and let it rest on the work surface. Proceed in the same way with the rest of the sheets.

9. When the fettuccine is all ready, you can cook them in the water that will have come to a boil. While the pasta is cooking, 2–3 minutes will be enough, prepare the sauce.

10. In a large frying pan, melt the butter over very low heat, taking care that it does not burn, and add a ladleful of the pasta cooking water: the starch it contains will help to make the sauce creamy.

11. Drain the fettuccine and add them directly into the pan with the butter. Pour another ladleful of cooking water and toss briefly, stirring quickly.

12. At this point, turn off the heat and add the grated Parmesan cheese; finally season with a pinch of salt and a generous grinding of black pepper and stir again to mix well the pasta with the sauce.

13. The fettuccine Alfredo is ready to be served.

TIPS:

In the United States you won't find a restaurant that doesn't offer fettuccine Alfredo!
It will be difficult to find one that follows the original recipe from the Alfredo restaurant in Rome. Many in fact add cream, which helps in the creation of the typical sauce. Don't worry, if you follow Grandma Lucia's recipe you won't need it!
I'll tell you also a curiosity: Alfredo di Lelio sold his restaurant in Via della Scrofa in Rome in 1943 and opened another one in 1950 with his son, "Il Vero Alfredo" in Piazza Augusto Imperatore 30, where fettuccine Alfredo is still made according to the original recipe, handed down from father to son, and served with gold cutlery donated by Mary Pickford and Douglas Fairbanks! If you are in Rome, you can't miss Alfredo's!

Ravioli con Ricotta e Spinaci
Ravioli Ricotta and Spinach

Ingredients to prepare 24 Ravioli

Dough	Seasoning after cooking
• 8.8 oz flour	• 1,75 oz butter
• 2 whole eggs	• 2 fresh sage leaflets
• 1 egg yolk	
• Semolina for sprinkling to taste	

Stuffing

- 8,8 oz spinach
- 4,4 oz ricotta
- 1,75 oz parmesan cheese
- Nutmeg to taste
- Salt to taste
- Black pepper to taste

DIRECTIONS:

1. Start by preparing the fresh egg pastry. Take the flour (leave about 1.7 oz aside to add as needed) and pour it into a bowl along with the eggs that you have previously beaten. Knead the ingredients well with your hands to create a homogeneous mixture. If the dough is not very elastic, add some warm water to make it softer and to be able to roll it out with a rolling pin or a pasta machine. If on the contrary, the dough is sticky, you can add the flour kept aside, slowly while you work the dough.
2. Transfer the dough onto a work surface and knead vigorously, when you have obtained a smooth and homogeneous dough, shape it into a ball and wrap it in cling film: let the dough rest for 30 minutes away from light and draughts that could dry it out.
3. While the pasta is resting dedicate yourself to the filling: take a non-stick pan, with a wide bottom, in which you will pour the rinsed spinach, cover them with the lid to let them wilt. Let them cook until soft, it will take about a couple of minutes. When softened, drain to remove excess liquid and set aside.
4. Take a large bowl and pour ricotta and Parmigiano. Flavor with grated nutmeg and, with the help of hand whips, mix the ingredients to combine them. Add salt and pepper.
5. When all the ingredients are mixed, chop the spinach in a blender and add it to the ricotta cream. Mix the ingredients well to obtain a homogeneous mixture. Transfer the mixture into a piping bag and set aside.
6. At this point, the pastry will have rested. Take it and divide it into 2 loaves. Wrap one in plastic wrap so that it doesn't dry out and lightly flour the other with flour (which won't be absorbed into the dough). Roll out the floured dough with the puff pastry machine passing it between the rollers from the widest to the penultimate narrowest thickness: you should obtain a rectangular pastry about 0.04 inches thick. Repeat the operation with the other roll.
7. Roll out one of the 2 pastry rectangles on a work surface lightly floured with semolina flour and create small mounds of filling with a piping bag. Arrange them about 1.15 inches apart.
8. With a finger, dirty the edges of the pastry with water (if you prefer you can also brush the edges with a kitchen brush) so that when you roll out the second pastry over it, it will stick more easily.
9. Roll out the second sheet over the first. Be careful to let the air escape between one ravioli and the other, pressing around the filling with your fingers, so as to prevent them from opening during cooking and letting the filling escape. This step is very important, pay attention. When you lay the second sheet of pastry, make the edges match the first.
10. Then, with a notched pasta cutter, cut out ravioli about 1.55x1.55 inches in size: you will obtain about 24 ravioli that you will place on a tray lightly floured with bran.
11. The ricotta and spinach ravioli are now ready! Cook them in salted boiling water for about 3–4 minutes.
12. In a separate pan pour the butter and the sage leaves, washed and dried well. Turn on medium-high heat and allow to melt.

13. Take the ravioli out of the cooking pot with the help of a slotted spoon and transfer them directly into the pan where the butter has melted.
14. Sauté for about 1 minute, and serve the ravioli still hot.

TIPS:

Having learned how to make perfect ravioli from this recipe, you can season the filling to your taste and imagination. For example, my grandmother used to make them stuffed with minced meat and ricotta cheese and at the end of cooking, she would dress them with a tomato sauce.

Spaghetti alla Carbonara
Spaghetti Carbonara

Servings: 4 people

Ingredients

- 12 oz spaghetti
- 5.3 oz pillow
- 6 egg yolks
- 1.75 oz pecorino Romano cheese
- Black pepper to taste
- Salt

DIRECTIONS:

1. Put a high-sided pot with salted water on the stove to cook the pasta.
2. In the meantime, remove the rind from the pillow and cut it first into slices and then into strips about 0.4 inches thick. Pour the pieces of pillow into a non-stick pan and brown for about 10 minutes over medium-high heat, being careful not to burn it otherwise it will release too strong an aroma.
3. Meanwhile, lower the spaghetti into the boiling water and cook them al dente.
4. Meanwhile, pour the egg yolks into a bowl. Add the grated Pecorino cheese and season with black pepper. Mix everything with a hand whisk until you obtain a smooth cream.
5. In the meantime, the pillow should be cooked; turn off the heat and, using a ladle, remove it from the pan, leaving the cooking liquid in the pan. Transfer the guanciale into a small bowl and set aside.
6. Pour a few tbsp of the cooking water into the pan along with the pillow fat.
7. Drain the pasta when al dente and transfer it directly to the pan with the cooking liquid. Saute briefly to add flavor. Remove from the heat and pour the egg and Pecorino mixture into the pan. Stir quickly to amalgamate. To make it creamy you can add a little of the pasta cooking water (if necessary).
8. Add the guanciale, mix one last time and immediately serve the spaghetti alla carbonara adding some pecorino cheese on top and a pinch of black pepper.

TIPS:

I recommend using fresh eggs and not browning the pillow too much, otherwise it may release a bitter taste.
Many people also use onion to flavor the pillow, if you like you can use it but the real traditional recipe does not include it and above all does not include cream.
Don't mention cream in carbonara to a Roman, you never know how he might react!

Orecchiette con Cime di Rapa
Orecchiette With Turnip Tops

Servings: 3 people

Ingredients

- 35 oz turnip tops
- 1.75 oz breadcrumbs
- Salt up to taste
- 1 garlic clove
- 2 anchovies in oil
- 3 tbsp extra virgin olive oil

Ingredients to prepare 10.5 oz of Orecchiette

- 3.5 oz warm water
- 3.5 oz re-milled durum wheat semolina
- Salt up to taste

DIRECTIONS:

1. To prepare the orecchiette, first, pour the re-milled durum wheat semolina flour onto the pastry board, form the typical fountain and add a pinch of salt to the flour. In the center pour the water at room temperature and start working with your fingers to incorporate the flour and work until you get a homogeneous and elastic dough. It will take about 10 minutes of working. Give the dough a round shape and cover it with a clean cloth: it should rest at room temperature for about 15 minutes.
2. After the resting time has passed, take out a piece of dough, while the rest you can leave covered by the dishcloth. Knead it into a loaf about 0.4 inches thick. Using the pastry cutter, cut out small pieces of about 0.4 inches.
3. With the help of a smooth-bladed knife, form shells by dragging each piece towards you on the pastry board. Then turn the shell over on itself. Continue until you have finished all the dough and arrange the ready orecchiette on a tray covered with a dish towel and lightly dusted with semolina.
4. For the dressing, remove the outer leaves from the turnip greens and remove only the inner leaves and flowers with a small knife (or your hands). Once ready, rinse, drain, dry well and set aside.
5. In the meantime, place on the stove a pot with other edges with plenty of water and salted to taste, which will be used to boil the turnip tops later.
6. In a large frying pan pour half the amount of oil and add the breadcrumbs, stir with a kitchen spatula and let it toast over medium heat until golden brown, then set aside.
7. As soon as the water comes to a boil, boil the turnip tops previously cleaned: they should cook for about 5 minutes.
8. In the meantime, prepare the sauté: in a frying pan pour the remaining oil, a clove of crushed garlic and the anchovy fillets drained from the preserving oil. Stir with a wooden spoon to dissolve the anchovies in the pan; it will only take a few minutes for the mixture to take on flavor and when it is ready, remove the garlic and turn off the heat.
9. After 5 minutes of cooking the turnip tops, add the orecchiette pasta to the same pan and cook for about 5 minutes more. Stir gently, then drain the orecchiette and turnip tops and pour them directly into the pan with the sauté.
10. Saute briefly and season with a pinch of salt; once ready, turn off the heat and serve the orecchiette with turnip tops, adding a drizzle of raw oil and toasted breadcrumbs at the last.

TIPS:

Orecchiette with turnip tops is one of the most representative dishes of Puglia. This first course is prepared throughout the region, even with accompaniments other than turnip greens such as broccoli or tomato sauce. I remember that my grandmother often dressed them with Ragù sauce and finally, once they were served, she would sprinkle them with a handful of Parmesan cheese. A real treat!

Gnocchi alla Sorrentina
Gnocchi alla Sorrentina

Servings: 4 people

For the gnocchi

- 35 oz red potatoes
- 10.6 oz flour
- 1 medium egg
- Salt up to taste
- Semolina to taste

For seasoning

- 8.8 oz mozzarella
- 2.5 oz grated parmesan cheese

For the tomato sauce

- 21.15 oz tomato sauce
- 6 leaves of basil
- 1 clove of garlic
- 2 tbsp extra virgin olive oil
- Salt up to taste

DIRECTIONS:

1. To prepare the gnocchi alla Sorrentina start with the potatoes: wash them under running water to remove any dirt, then pour them into a large saucepan, add the water to cover them completely, and cook them for about 30–40 minutes (depending on the size the time may vary, check with a fork, the potatoes will be cooked when they are soft to the center).
2. In the meantime, prepare the sauce: in a high-sided pan, pour the oil, the peeled clove of garlic and the tomato puree, add a pinch of salt to taste; season with the basil leaves, then cover with the lid and let the sauce cook over medium-low heat for about 30 minutes.
3. When the potatoes are ready, drain them well.
4. Now sift the flour on the pastry board and create the classic fountain (a pyramid of flour with a deep hole in the center), mash the potatoes still hot with a potato masher in the center of the fountain of flour (or peel and mash them by hand first).
5. Pour the egg and salt over the potatoes, then start to knead: this operation should be done rather quickly, just enough time to compact the dough and give it a smooth and soft consistency (not sticky but not too tough either). Cover the dough with a clean, dry cloth.
6. Boil water in a large saucepan to cook the gnocchi and add a pinch of salt.
7. In the meantime, gradually take a portion of dough, keeping the remaining one covered, and make some bigoli (cylinders of dough, like snakes) about 1 inch thick. Sprinkle with a little semolina and cut the gnocchi out of each strand using a knife. To give the classic ridge to the gnocchi you can use a gnocchi cutter or you can make them smooth using your index finger. As you prepare them, place them on a tray lined with a clean cloth and lightly sprinkled with semolina.
8. Once ready, remove the garlic from the sauce and pour most of it into a very large bowl.
9. Boil the gnocchi by pouring them into the pan at least 2–3 times; they will have to cook for a few moments, taking care that the water in the pan is not quite boiling to avoid ruining them: drain the gnocchi with the aid of a slotted spoon as soon as they rise to the surface and then gradually plunge them into the bowl where you have poured the sauce. Stir gently with a spoon.
10. In a fairly large baking dish, pour the remaining sauce over the bottom and pour in the gnocchi as well.
11. Season with a layer of diced mozzarella and a sprinkling of Parmigiano. Continue with another layer of gnocchi, the remaining mozzarella and Parmigiano.
12. Bake the gnocchi alla Sorrentina in a static oven preheated to 480°F on grill mode for 5 minutes.
13. Serve them piping hot!

Zuppa di Pesce
Fish Soup

Servings: 6 people

Ingredients

- 6 prawns
- 14 oz cuttlefish (cleaned)
- oz hen (to be cleaned)
- 17.5 oz monkfish tail (to be cleaned)
- 17.5 oz mullet (to be cleaned)
- Extra virgin olive oil to taste
- 2 cloves of garlic
- Parsley to taste
- 0.3 cup white wine
- Salt up to taste
- Black pepper to taste
- 17.5 oz tomato puree
- 1 stalk celery
- 1 carrot
- 1 white onion
- 0.4 gal water
- White peppercorns (or black pepper) to taste
- Parsley to taste

For the mussels

- 35 oz mussels
- Extra virgin olive oil to taste
- 1 clove of garlic

DIRECTIONS:

1. To make the chowder, start by cleaning the chickens: after having eviscerated and rinsed them, cut into the back at the height of the central bone and divide into two fillets, then remove the smaller bones with the special kitchen pliers; keep the fillet lying on the cut and rub it with your fingertips to identify the bones. Keep the scraps as you will need them for the broth.
2. Now prepare the mullet: after having gutted and rinsed them, remove the head and tail, cut into the back and cut out two fillets, eliminating the central bone. Here too, eliminate the bones with pliers. Keep the scraps.
3. Clean the monkfish: gut it, remove the tail and fins, peel off the skin and cut with a knife all along the back, next to the central bone, cut out the fillet and cut it into slices. Always keep the scraps aside.
4. Clean the shrimp: remove the head and tail, remove the carapace and extract the intestines on the back using a toothpick.
5. Wash the vegetables for the fish stock and cut them into chunks.
6. In a large saucepan with high sides pour the vegetables, the parsley, the scraps from the cleaning of the fish and the peppercorns, you can choose to use the black or white one.
7. Cover with water, turn on the heat and cook for 2 hours from boiling. While cooking, remove the foam that forms on the surface with a skimmer.
8. Clean the mussels: make sure they are all closed, the broken or open ones must be discarded. Carefully clean the shell with a small knife, remove the barb and, finally, scrape away the impurities with a clean straw. Rinse them carefully.
9. In a high-sided pan heat a little oil with a clove of garlic. Pour in the mussels and cover with a lid. Cook for 3–4 minutes, shaking the pan from time to time. The mussels should be all open. Use a colander to collect their cooking water and keep it aside. Then shell them, taking care to set aside a few mussels with their shells for garnishing the dishes.
10. Now cut the cuttlefish into strips. In a large saucepan, heat a little oil with 2 cloves of garlic, add the cuttlefish and fry over high heat for 3–4 minutes. Deglaze with the white wine and let it evaporate.
11. Pour in the tomato puree and the cooking water from the mussels. Cover with the lid and cook for 25 minutes on a low flame.
12. Meanwhile, the fish stock will be ready, strain it through a colander and keep it aside.
13. Remove the garlic cloves from the soup, add the slices of monkfish and 28 oz of the fish stock you prepared. Cook over low heat for 10 minutes.
14. At this point, add the gurnard and mullet fillets and continue cooking for a further 5 minutes, turning the pan so as not to flake the fish. Finally pour in the prawns and shelled mussels.
15. Taste, add salt and pepper just now, let it season for another minute, then turn off the heat.
16. Serve the soup on a plate and place the mussels with their shells on top, sprinkle with chopped parsley and serve the fish soup piping hot.

Lasagne al Forno
Lasagne in the Oven

Servings: 8 people

For the lasagna
- 8.8 oz grated parmesan cheese
- 20–22 sheets of egg lasagne

For the Bolognese Ragout
- 24.5 oz ground beef (you can also add pork if you wish)
- ½ onion
- 0.6 cup white wine
- 1 stalk celery
- 2 carrots
- 29 oz tomato sauce
- 2 tbsp milk (if desired)
- 3 tbsp extra virgin olive oil
- Salt to taste

For the béchamel
- 3.5 oz flour
- 4 cups whole milk
- 3.5 oz butter
- Nutmeg (to grate) to taste
- 1 pinch salt

For seasoning
- 7 oz cooked ham (sliced)
- 7 oz mozzarella (well drained)

DIRECTIONS:

1. Prepare the Ragù first as it needs a longer cooking time: Clean the celery and carrots, wash under running water and chop finely with a knife along with the onion.

2. Then prepare the classic soffritto: pour the olive oil into a high-sided pan, heat, add the chopped mixture and fry for a few minutes, stirring. Once the sauté is wilted, add the chopped meat that you are going to separate with the help of a fork and let it brown for a few minutes. When the meat is dry, pour in the white wine. Let the alcohol evaporate and then add the tomato puree. Adjust the salt and cook over medium heat for about 2 hours with the lid slightly open. Stir from time to time and add a little water if needed in case the sauce is too dry. To make the sauce more delicate, you can add milk at the end of cooking if you like.

3. Prepare the homemade béchamel: Melt the butter in small pieces over low heat in a saucepan and then, removing it from the heat, add the sifted flour. Stir vigorously with a whisk to remove lumps and place the pan back on the heat until the mixture is golden brown. Incorporate the milk (even warm is fine, the important thing is that it is not cold) and work the mixture with a hand whisk to avoid lumps. Adjust the salt and add grated nutmeg and, stirring continuously with the whisk, cook the béchamel until it is thick and full-bodied. It will smell delicious.

4. Now it is time to assemble the baked lasagne: Cut the mozzarella and cooked ham into small pieces.

5. Spread a ladleful of béchamel sauce on the bottom of a rectangular baking dish of about 12×8 inches. Lay the lasagna sheets over the entire surface and top with béchamel sauce, a few ladles of meat sauce, a little mozzarella, a little ham and grated Parmesan cheese. Cover with other sheets and proceed in layers until you run out of ingredients. Finish with a layer of lasagna topped with plenty of meat sauce and sprinkled with Parmesan cheese.

6. Bake in a preheated 350ºF oven for about 30 minutes, until a delicious golden crust forms on the surface. Remove from oven and let cool for about 5 minutes.

7. The baked lasagna is now ready to serve.

Spaghetti al Pomodoro Fresco
Spaghetti With Fresh Tomatoes

Servings: 4 people

Ingredients

- 17.5 oz fresh red cherry tomatoes
- 2 tbsp olive oil
- ½ red onion
- Basil
- 13 oz Spaghetti
- Ice to taste

DIRECTIONS:

1. Take a high-sided pot, fill it with water, and put it on a high flame.
2. In the meantime, take the cherry tomatoes and make a small cross-shaped incision, using a knife, on the top of the tomato.
3. When the water boils, pour the cherry tomatoes inside and cook for about 2 minutes.
4. Meanwhile, take a bowl that can hold the cherry tomatoes and fill it with ice and 2 glasses of water.
5. Once the 2 minutes have passed, take the cherry tomatoes with the help of a slotted spoon and quickly pour them into the bowl with the ice. This will stop the cooking process of the cherry tomatoes and you can easily remove the peel. With the help of a knife, gently remove the peel, cut them in half and keep them aside.
6. Take a pot to cook the pasta in, fill it with water, add salt, and bring it to a boil.
7. In the meantime, pour the olive oil into a pan; peel and chop the onion into small pieces and add it to the oil. Fry for about 2 minutes, stirring occasionally. As soon as the onion is ready, add the cherry tomatoes and mix quickly so that they do not stick together. With the help of a fork lightly crush the tomatoes, add a pinch of salt to taste, and cook for a couple of minutes then turn off the heat.
8. As soon as the water boils, drop the pasta and drain when al dente, keeping aside a cup of cooking water. Pour the pasta into the pan of cherry tomatoes, use a high flame. Add the cooking water and sauté until the water is absorbed.
9. Turn off and season everything with the washed and dried basil leaves.
10. Serve and enjoy the freshness of this fresh and flavorful dish.

TIPS:

My family has always liked the skin of cherry tomatoes. In fact, they've never cooked them without; this is a recipe I make because my kids don't like the skin on the tomatoes, so to get them to eat them, I added this process to peel them.
If you like tomato skins, you can skip the initial process and just add the cherry tomatoes to the pan with the oil and onion, washing, drying and cutting them in half. You'll just need to cook them for a few minutes before you can mash them and continue with the cooking process as per the procedure.

Cannelloni al Forno
Baked Cannelloni

Servings: 2 people

**For the egg pasta
(for 8 cannelloni)**
- 3.5 oz flour
- 1 medium egg

For the béchamel
- 3.5 oz whole milk
- 0,7 oz butter
- 0.7 oz flour
- Nutmeg grated to taste
- 1 pinch salt

For seasoning
- Grated parmesan cheese

For the stuffing
- 7 oz sausage
- 10,5 oz minced beef
- 3.5 oz grated parmesan cheese
- 1 tbsp extra virgin olive oil
- 1 onion
- 1 stalk celery
- 1 carrot
- 0.3 cup red wine
- 1 pinch fine salt
- 1 pinch black pepper
- 10.5 oz tomato puree

DIRECTIONS:

1. Clean and finely chop celery, carrot and onion.
2. Remove the casing from the sausage and shred it with a knife. Now move to the stove.
3. In a frying pan pour the olive oil and then add the chopped sausage, let it brown well. When it is well browned add the chopped vegetables and stir, let it stew for 5–6 minutes.
4. Add the ground beef, separate it with the help of a fork, stir and turn up the flame. Let it brown unhurriedly for a couple of minutes. Deglaze with the red wine and stir again.
5. As soon as the alcohol has evaporated add the tomato puree. Stir to incorporate it and rinse the container that contained the puree with a little water to collect the surplus and add the water from the container to the sauce (fill the container halfway); add a pinch of salt to taste. Cover with a lid leaving a small vent and cook for 1 hour. Check from time to time.
6. Now prepare the egg pasta. Pour the flour into a bowl and add the slightly beaten egg. Work the dough with your hands until the ingredients are mixed.
7. Transfer the dough to a pastry board and knead it again until you get a smooth and homogeneous, firm and elastic mixture, which will give a spherical shape. At this point wrap it with plastic wrap and let it rest for about 1 hour in a cool, dry place so that it acquires the right elasticity.
8. Prepare the béchamel sauce. Melt the butter in small pieces over gentle heat in a saucepan and then, removing it from the heat, add the sifted flour. Stir vigorously with a whisk to eliminate lumps and return the pan to heat until the mixture is golden brown. Incorporate the milk (even lukewarm is fine, the important thing is that it is not cold from the fridge) and work the mixture with a hand whisk to avoid lumps. Adjust the salt and add grated nutmeg and, stirring continuously with the whisk, cook the béchamel until it is thick and full-bodied.
9. Transfer the béchamel sauce to a glass bowl and cover with cling film. Once cold, if it is too thick, add a little milk.
10. Take the loaf of egg pasta that has rested and reached the right elasticity and divide it in two. Roll out each part of dough with the sheeter starting from the widest width to the narrowest. You will obtain a sheet about 0.08 inches thick. If you don't have a rolling machine, you can roll out the dough by hand, using a lightly floured rolling pin. At the end cut out 8 rectangles 4 x 5.5 inches each.
11. Once you have obtained the rectangles of dough, you will have to blanch them one at a time for a maximum of 1 minute in lightly salted boiling water. Drain them and transfer them to a tray where you will have placed a dish towel; it is important to stretch perfectly the various rectangles without overlapping them.
12. Meanwhile, the ragu will be ready and cooled, set aside 8.8 oz.
13. Add the grated cheese to the remaining meat sauce and season with pepper. Mix and place in the fridge.

14. Take a rectangle of dough and stuff it with the meat sauce on one side only, then roll the pastry over itself. Seal the dough to form filled cylinders.
15. Spread 2–3 tbsp of béchamel sauce in the bottom of an approximately 8 x 12-inch baking dish. Place the cannelloni on top. Top them with the remaining béchamel sauce and meat sauce kept aside, the grated cheese and bake in a static oven preheated to 400°F for 15 minutes on the medium rack and 5 minutes at 465°F, in grill mode, on the slightly higher rack, until golden brown.
16. All you have left to do is serve your homemade cannelloni still warm! Delicious!

TIPS:

Again, as with the ravioli, you can indulge yourself as you see fit for the cannelloni filling.
I also make them stuffed with ricotta cheese, spinach, and sausage, or with ricotta cheese, mushrooms, and minced meat; either way they will always be delicious!

Sartù di Riso
Neapolitan Rice Timbale

Servings: 8 people

For a mold of 8 inches wide and 4.5 inches high
- 17–18 oz Carnaroli rice
- 7 oz frozen peas
- 2 hard-boiled eggs
- 5.3 oz mozzarella
- Salt up to taste
- 2 eggs

For the Ragù alla Napoletana
- 25 oz rib eye
- 1 golden onion
- 3 tbsp extra virgin olive oil
- 25 oz tomato puree
- 0.3 cup red wine
- 1.25 cups water

For 100 patties (0.14 oz each)
- 7 oz ground beef
- 2.6 oz bread only stale crumbs
- 1 egg
- 1 oz Parmigiano Reggiano DOP to grate
- Salt up to taste
- Black pepper to taste
- 1 tsp chopped parsley
- Peanut seed oil for frying

For the mold
- Butter to taste
- Breadcrumbs to taste

DIRECTIONS:

1. To prepare the rice sartù start by preparing the classic Neapolitan meat sauce. Then in a very large pan with high sides, sauté a chopped onion on a low flame, then add all the pieces of meat for a few minutes and brown them on all sides. Deglaze with the wine. As soon as the alcohol has evaporated completely, pour in the tomato puree, the water and a pinch of salt. Leave to cook over low heat: the sauce should simmer for at least 4 hours, adding more water if too dry. At the end of cooking make sure that the meat sauce has just the right amount of salt and set the pieces of meat aside (you can serve it as a second course, accompanying it with a side dish of vegetables).

2. To prepare the meatballs, start by soaking the bread crumbs in cold water for about 10 minutes, then drain and squeeze well, with a fork or with your hands, to remove all the excess water.

3. In a bowl pour the minced meat together with the slightly beaten egg, the Parmesan cheese and the well-squeezed breadcrumbs, season with salt and pepper and add the chopped parsley. Knead until you obtain a homogeneous mixture. At this point you can form the meatballs: take about 0.14 oz of dough and shape it in your hands to obtain small balls. By doing this you will obtain about 100 patties.

4. Heat some peanut oil in a frying pan: you don't want to do an immersion cooking so don't pour a lot. When the oil is hot, start placing the patties in the pan a little at a time, cooking them for about 3 minutes and turning them halfway through cooking. Once ready, place them on a sheet of paper towels and continue like this with the others.

5. Finally, proceed with the last step to prepare the Sartù di Riso. First, prepare the hard-boiled eggs. Fill a saucepan with water and as soon as it comes to a boil, immerse the eggs and cook them for 9 minutes. Then drain them, pass them under fresh water for a few moments and begin to peel them. Finally, slice them thinly with a knife.

6. Put the Neapolitan ragout back on the flame, add 7 oz of water and cook the rice in the sauce. Then add salt to taste and cook over medium-low heat, stirring occasionally so that the rice does not stick to the bottom. The rice should completely absorb the water.

7. When it is cooked, transfer it to a bowl and let it cool for about 10 minutes.

8. In the meantime, beat the eggs in a bowl together with salt, pepper and grated cheese. Mix everything well and pour over the now warmed rice and continue stirring to incorporate all the ingredients.

9. Now grease an 8-inch diameter, 5-inch high mold with butter; then sprinkle with breadcrumbs and pour a little of the rice mixture, taking care to spread it all around, crushing it with the back of a spoon as you go, so as to create a coating about 0.4 inches thick. Make sure to keep some of the rice aside to seal the timbale.

10. At this point, you can proceed to stuff the timballo, but first cut the mozzarella into cubes.

11. In the center of the sartù lay a first layer of hard-boiled eggs and mozzarella, then the peas (just leave them at room temperature while you're preparing the rest), and finally the meatballs; continue in this way by adding layers of mozzarella, peas and meatballs.

12. Finally, cover the last layer with sliced eggs and the remaining rice, which you will level with a spoon in order to compact the surface.
13. Sprinkle with breadcrumbs and add a few knobs of butter, then bake the timballo in a preheated, hot oven in static mode at 350°F for 60 minutes (cooking in fan mode is not recommended as it may dry out the mixture too much).
14. Leave to cool for about ten minutes before unmoulding the Sartù di Riso and enjoy it warm.

TIPS:

I suggest you prepare the Neapolitan ragout in advance, even the day before if you prefer so that you don't have too many preparations to do at the same time. If you want to keep the timballo you can cover it with plastic wrap and leave it in the fridge for 1–2 days at most.

Risotto alla Pescatora
Risotto With Pescatora

Servings: 4 people

Ingredients
- 12.5 oz Carnaroli rice
- 1 shallot
- 0.6 cup white wine
- 7 oz gutted mullet
- 35 oz clams
- 17 oz calamari (already cleaned, only the mantle)
- 9 oz prawns
- Extra virgin olive oil to taste
- 1 garlic clove

For the tomato coulis
- 9 oz cherry tomatoes
- 1 pinch of sugar

- 1 pinch of fine salt
- 0.2 cup water
- 1 clove of garlic

For the broth
- 8 cups ice water
- 2 oz shallot
- 7 oz fennel
- black pepper in grains
- 2 leaves basil
- 2 garlic cloves

For the risotto mantecatura
- 3.5 oz extra virgin olive oil
- 0.15 oz fresh chili
- 5 leaves basil
- 1 pinch white pepper

DIRECTIONS:

1. First of all, take care of cleaning the clams. Make sure that all of them are well closed, otherwise discard the open ones. Transfer them to a bowl with water and salt for a couple of hours. Then drain them and start cooking them.
2. In a pan pour a little oil and let it heat over medium heat, then add a clove of crushed garlic and as soon as the oil is hot pour the well-drained clams. Turn up the heat, wait a few seconds and then pour in the white wine. Cover with a lid and cook for a few minutes until all the clams have opened.
3. At this point, using a colander, strain the clam cooking water into a bowl and set aside.
4. Shell the clams and keep them aside.
5. Move on to the squid. Cut the mantle (on the long side) in half with a knife with a smooth blade, open it and lay it on a cutting board and make very thin strips, as if they were threads. Set aside and take care of the mullet.
6. Cut off the head and the end of the tail of the mullet, then fillet the fish so as to obtain 2 regular fillets. Keep the scraps because you will need them to make the broth.
7. Now clean the prawns. Using your hands, remove the head and carapace together with the tail and remove, with the help of a toothpick, the intestine on the back. The scraps of shrimp will also be used to enrich the broth.
8. At this point, switch to the broth. Finely chop the shallot and cut the fennel into thin strips.
9. In a fairly large saucepan pour a little oil. Add 2 cleaned garlic cloves, the shallot, the shrimp shells and the bones of the mullet. Leave to brown for a few minutes, then add the iced water, fennel, peppercorns and basil leaves. Add the previously filtered water from the clams. Bring to a boil, then lower the heat and leave to cook for 15–18 minutes over a low flame.
10. Meanwhile, move on to the tomato coulis. In a saucepan pour the tomatoes, sugar, salt, poached garlic clove and water. Wait until it starts to boil, then cook for 5–6 minutes. At this point remove the garlic, turn off the heat and transfer everything to a blender. Blend everything and transfer it to a bowl. At this point also the broth will be ready, filter it eliminating all the waste, and keep it warm.
11. Now cook the rice. In a large frying pan pour a little oil, add the chopped shallot and let it wilt slightly.
12. Add the Carnaroli rice and, stirring occasionally, toast it. To understand when the rice is well toasted, touch it with the back of your hand, without burning yourself, and if it is hot, add the white wine, about 1.4 oz will be needed. As soon as the alcohol has evaporated, wet the rice with a couple of ladles of hot stock.
13. As soon as it starts to boil it will take about 13 minutes to cook, you will need to add more stock only as needed.
14. After about 10 minutes the rice will be almost cooked, add the clams and stir.
15. Then add the squid, stir again, add the shrimp and stir again.
16. Once the 13 minutes are up, turn off the heat and stir in the rice. Add the oil, the thinly sliced chili pepper, a grating of white pepper and a few basil leaves broken up with your hands.

17. Add the tomato coulis, stir, shaking the pan at the same time, so that the risotto is creamy.
18. Cover with a lid and leave it to rest for a minute and in the meantime quickly blanch the mullet. Pour a little oil into a pan, let it heat up and then add the mullet fillets. After a few seconds turn them over and finish cooking them on the other side. It will take a few seconds to cook them. Then place them on a tray with paper towels to dry them.
19. Take the rice and taste it. Adjust the salt and white pepper and if it is not creamy enough add a little more oil. Stir-fry one last time before serving.
20. Pour a ladleful of rice into the center of a plate. Tap with the palm of your hand under the bottom of the plate so that the rice is evenly distributed. Place 3 fillets of mullet on each portion.
21. Serve the risotto alla pescatora still hot, bon appetit!

TIPS:

The iced water added to make the broth allows for a thermal shock and thus extracts all the juices from the shells and waste from the fish. I recommend using it well iced. The quick cooking of the broth will allow you to keep all the flavors intact, with a less cloudy end result. The ladles of broth must be added with criteria: the rice must always be well visible and never completely covered.

Moreover, for this preparation, you will need only the squid's mantle, in case you bought them whole you can use the clumps frying them to serve them as a tasty second course.

Before frying them in seed oil, dip them in flour to create a delicious golden crust on the outside.

Tortellini in Brodo
Tortellini in Broth

Servings: 4 people

For the tortellini sheet
- 10.6 oz flour
- 3 medium eggs

For the tortellini stuffing
- 3.5 oz pork loin (single piece)
- 3.5 oz mortadella (single piece)
- 3.5 oz raw ham (single piece)
- 5.3 oz parmesan cheese pdo
- 1 egg
- Salt up to taste
- Nutmeg to taste

For the broth
- 1 white onion
- Cloves to taste
- 1 carrot
- 2 stalks of celery
- 1 gal cold water
- ½ hen
- 50 oz rib eye
- Salt to taste

DIRECTIONS:

1. To prepare the tortellini in broth, start with the filling, which will need a long rest. Cut the mortadella, ham, and loin into pieces, removing the tougher external parts.
2. Pass it through the meat grinder, using a medium mold and scooping the shredded meat into a bowl. Don't set the meat grinder aside, you'll need it again.
3. Add the grated cheese, salt, pepper and egg to the ground meat. Also, add a pinch of grated nutmeg. Mix all the ingredients by kneading with your hands.
4. Pass the mixture through the mincer again, this time using the thinner mold. Compact again with your hands, then cover with plastic wrap and refrigerate for 12 hours (so I recommend preparing the filling the day before).
5. When it's about 4 hours before the stuffing rests, prepare the meat stock. Peel the onion and cut it in half. Place 3 cloves on each half and place the onions in a hot pan.
6. Wash the celery and carrot well, then cut them into pieces.
7. Pour the chicken and beef into a large pot. Also, add celery and carrots.
8. When the onions are well browned move them to the pot with the meat. Add the water and a pinch of salt. Cook over medium heat. From boiling it will take about 4 hours of cooking.
9. In the meantime, prepare the egg pasta. Pour the flour onto a pastry board and make the classic fountain shape. Pour in the slightly beaten eggs and start mixing the ingredients with a fork.
10. Then knead by hand, continue until you get a smooth dough. Wrap it in plastic wrap and let it rest for 30 minutes at room temperature.
11. Occasionally check the broth and remove the foam using a skimmer.
12. Take the egg pasta and transfer it to a pastry board. Crush it with your hands to flatten it, then roll it out with a rolling pin until you get a very thin sheet.
13. Using a pastry cutter, cut out small squares. Place a tip of filling in the center of each square (you can help yourself with a teaspoon or a sac-a´ poche).
14. Lift one square, close it so that it forms a triangle and press lightly on the edges. Now pull down the two side edges, making them go around your finger. Seal by pinching the 2 edges of dough, and the first tortellino is ready. Do the same for all the others and gradually arrange them on a tray with a dish towel.
15. When the broth is ready, remove the meat and vegetables with a skimmer. Transfer them to a bowl. Taste the broth and adjust the salt if necessary. Then strain it, dividing the broth into two pots. Bring one of the two pots with the broth back to a boil and keep the other one warm. As soon as the broth in one pot starts to boil, submerge the tortellini. Wait a few minutes until they rise to the surface, then use a skimmer to scoop out a portion of tortellini and transfer it to a plate.
16. Add the hot broth, taking it from the other pot, this way it will be clearer.
17. Do the same until all the dishes are finished and serve the broth piping hot.

Tagliatelle alla Boscaiola
Tagliatelle Boscaiola Style

Servings: 4 people

Ingredients

- 13 oz egg noodles
- 13 oz porcini mushrooms
- 9 oz sausage
- 0.8 cup cooking cream
- 1 golden onion
- A few leaves of parsley
- 2 tbsp extra virgin olive oil
- Salt to taste

DIRECTIONS:

1. First, clean the mushrooms (not with water) and remove the stem end. With a kitchen brush, remove all earthy residue. If soil remains, wipe the surface of the mushroom with a dry cloth. Cut the mushrooms into vertical slices.
2. Take a pot with high sides, fill it with water and salt and put it on the stove to cook the noodles.
3. Chop the onion and sauté it in a frying pan with the oil for a few minutes, until just golden.
4. Add the sausage stripped of its casing and break it up with a fork. Let it brown for a few minutes, until it changes color.
5. Add the mushrooms, mix carefully and add a pinch of salt. Cover with a lid and continue cooking for 10 minutes, stirring occasionally. If necessary, add a few tbsp of the cooking water.
6. When cooked, taste and add salt to taste, add the cream and sprinkle with chopped parsley. Stir well. The Boscaiola sauce is ready!
7. In the meantime, the water for the pasta will have come to a boil and you can lower the noodles. When the pasta is cooked al dente, drain it and pour it into the pan with the sauce.
8. Mix everything together and serve on various plates. The Tagliatelle alla Boscaiola are ready... how delicious!

TIPS:

If it's not porcini mushroom season, you can use any type of mushroom, even champignons which are there all year round. Alternatively, you can use frozen porcini mushrooms (11oz).
You can replace the sausage with equal amounts of diced bacon.
If you don't like cream, you can replace it with 5.3 oz of Philadelphia cheese, which you will melt together with the mushrooms and sausage, with a little cooking water. The result will be creamy!

Risotto allo Zafferano
Saffron Risotto

Servings: 4 people

Ingredients

- 1 tsp saffron in pistils
- 11.5 oz Carnaroli rice
- 4.4 oz butter
- 1 onion
- 2.8 oz Grana Padano DOP for grating
- 0.3 cup white wine
- 0.2–0.3 gal vegetable stock
- Salt up to taste

To garnish

- Saffron pistils to taste

DIRECTIONS:

1. To make saffron risotto (or Milanese risotto), first put the pistils in a small glass, pour enough water over them to cover the pistils completely, stir and leave to infuse overnight, so the pistils will release all their color.
2. Then prepare a light vegetable broth as I have already explained in other recipes, for this recipe you will need one liter.
3. Finely chop the onion so that it can melt while cooking and not be felt while tasting the risotto.
4. In a large saucepan pour 1.75 oz of butter taken from the total amount needed, melt it over gentle heat, then pour the chopped onion and let it stew for 10–15 minutes adding some broth to keep the sauté from drying out: the onion should be very transparent and soft.
5. Once the onion is stewed, pour in the rice and toast it for 3–4 minutes, so the grains will seal and hold the cooking well. Deglaze with the white wine and let it evaporate completely.
6. At this point, continue cooking for about 18–20 minutes, adding the broth one ladle at a time as it is absorbed by the rice: the grains should always be covered.
7. 5 minutes before the rice is cooked, pour in the water with the saffron pistils you had infused, stir to flavor and tint the risotto a nice golden color.
8. Once cooked, turn off the heat, taste and season, and season with grated cheese and the remaining 2.65 oz of butter, stir and cover with the lid and let stand for a couple of minutes.
9. At this point the saffron risotto is ready, serve piping hot garnishing the dish with a few more pistils.

TIPS:

My grandmother used to tell me this story: saffron, a very precious and also very expensive spice, was used in 1754 to prepare a yellow risotto for a wedding dinner.
At that time Mastro Valerio di Fiandra was working on the decoration of the stained-glass windows of the Duomo of Milan and was helped by an assistant who was called Zafferano, because he used to make the colors brighter by adding spice.
One day the master, as a joke, told Zafferano that with his mania he would incorporate saffron into his food as well. So, on the day of the wedding of the daughter of Valerio di Fiandra, Zafferano convinced the cook to incorporate the spice into the risotto he was preparing. The dish was presented at the banquet and the yellow risotto was a success, especially for its color and tasty flavor.

SECONDS AND SIDE DISHES

Polpette Fritte
Fried Meatballs

Servings: 4 people

Ingredients

- 18 oz ground beef
- 9 oz stale bread
- Parsley
- 1 garlic clove
- 5.5 oz parmesan cheese
- 1.5 oz pine nuts
- 2 eggs
- 1 tbsp olive oil
- Sunflower or peanut oil
- Salt and pepper to taste

DIRECTIONS:

1. Soak the stale bread in water, when it is soft remove the crust and crumble it into a bowl making sure to have wrung well to remove the water.
2. Add to the bread the minced beef, eggs, Parmesan cheese, salt, pepper, parsley washed and chopped, garlic that you have previously crushed into pulp (you can also use garlic powder, in this case, ½ tsp will be fine), olive oil and pine nuts previously toasted and coarsely chopped.
3. Mix everything with your hands until the dough is smooth and neither too wet nor dry.
4. Take a baking tray and cover it with baking paper.
5. With a spoon, help yourself to a portion of the dough, and with wet hands create a meatball. Crush the meatball between your palms and place it on the baking tray. Continue like this until the dough is finished.
6. Prepare a frying pan and pour enough seed oil to cover half the height of the meatballs being cooked. Put it on heat and bring the oil to 180°F.
7. Lay the meatballs gently in the hot oil.
8. As soon as one side is golden brown, flip them over and cook the other side as well.
9. Once cooked, place them on a tray covered with paper towels to remove excess oil.

TIPS:

I advise you to eat the meatballs while they are still hot so that you can taste all the flavors, but they are also excellent cold. I still remember when grandma Lucia used to prepare them and I used to secretly steal them from the plate while they were still hot; I always burned my tongue because they were so hot but the taste was irresistible.

Polpette al Sugo
Meatballs With Sauce

Servings: 4 people

Ingredients

- 18 oz ground beef
- 9 oz stale bread
- Parsley
- 2 garlic cloves
- 1 carrot
- 1 tuft of basil
- 21 oz tomato puree
- 1.5 cups water
- 5 oz Parmesan cheese
- 1,5 oz pine nuts
- 2 eggs
- 3 tbsp olive oil
- Salt and pepper to taste

DIRECTIONS:

1. Start by making the sauce. Pour 2 tbsp of olive oil into a high-sided pot.
2. Clean the garlic clove and carrot and chop them into small pieces.
3. When the oil is hot pour in the garlic and onion and sauté for a minute. Move the pot from the heat and add the tomato puree, water, basil leaves and salt. Move the pot back to the heat and cover with a lid.
4. Now prepare the meatballs. The procedure is the same as the fried ones, but in this case, you will avoid frying. Soak the stale bread in water, when it is soft remove the crust and crumble it into a bowl making sure to have wrung well to remove water.
5. Add to the bread the mince, eggs, Parmesan cheese, salt, pepper, washed and chopped parsley, 1 clove of garlic that you have previously crushed into pulp (you can also use garlic powder, in this case, 1 tsp will be fine), a tbsp of olive oil and the pine nuts previously toasted and coarsely chopped.
6. Mix everything with your hands until the mixture is smooth and neither too wet nor too dry. With a spoon, help yourself to a portion of the mixture and with wet hands create a meatball. Lightly crush the patty between your palms and gently place it in the pan of sauce. Continue like this until the dough is finished.
7. Stir the sauce gently and cook for at least 2 hours and 30 minutes, over low heat, making sure the sauce doesn't get too dry otherwise you might burn the meatballs.

TIPS:

I remember that when my grandmother prepared meatballs with sauce, there was always a lot of sauce left over and she used it the next day to season pasta or rice. She always added a little bit of ricotta cheese too. It was delicious. So, if you have a leftover sauce, you can safely use it within a maximum of 24–48 hours, storing it in the covered pot at room temperature.

Parmigiana di Melanzane
Eggplant Parmigiana

Servings: 8 people

Ingredients

- 60 oz eggplants
- 35 oz tomato puree
- 17 oz fiordilatte
- 5 oz parmesan cheese pdo
- 1 onion
- Basil to taste
- 1 tbsp extra virgin olive oil
- Black pepper to taste
- Salt up to taste

For frying

- Peanut seed oil to taste

DIRECTIONS:

1. Start by making the sauce. Peel and chop the onion.
2. Take a large pot and pour the olive oil and let it heat up, then add the onion. Let it brown for a couple of minutes, stirring often so that it doesn't burn, then add the tomato puree. Season with salt and add the basil leaves; rinse the tomato puree container with water, shake it and pour the contents into the pot, then leave to cook over low heat for 45–50 minutes.
3. In the meantime, cut the fiordilatte into cubes, keeping aside a piece that will be used at the end. Drain the cubes in a colander placed in a bowl, cover with plastic wrap and set aside: this process serves to remove excess whey.
4. Prepare the eggplants, wash, dry and remove the core.
5. Slice them lengthwise into 0.16-inch thick slices.
6. Prepare a pan with the seed oil (consider that the oil will have to completely cover the eggplant slice).
7. Fry the eggplants in pre-heated oil, dipping a few pieces at a time, as soon as they are lightly browned place them on a tray with absorbent paper. When there is no more space on the tray, place more blotting paper on the eggplants already fried and add the last pieces on top of them.
8. Make up the parmigiana. Start by pouring some of the sauce into an 8 x 12-inch baking dish.
9. Form the first layer by arranging the slices of eggplant, pour a ladle of tomato sauce, spread it over the entire layer of eggplant and distribute some cubes of fiordilatte and sprinkle with grated Parmigiano.
10. Start adding the eggplants in the opposite direction to the previous ones, the tomato sauce, and then the cheeses again. Go on like this until you get to the last layer of eggplants that you will season, once again, with tomato sauce, the fiordilatte cheese that you have kept aside, to be broken up by hand and the basil.
11. Finish with grated Parmesan cheese and bake in a static oven, already heated to 400°F, for about 30 minutes.
12. Once the cooking time has elapsed, leave to rest for 15–20 minutes before serving the aubergine parmigiana as a side dish.

TIPS:

My grandmother used to say that there is nothing better than a slice of eggplant parmigiana to cheer you up.
This recipe is contested as its origins from the north to the south of Italy: In this case the recipe is from Campania, the simplest one. Few ingredients such as tomato, eggplant, basil and cheese, a lot of flavors for a dish symbol of Mediterranean cuisine!
In case you have leftovers, you can store them in the fridge, covered with foil, for up to 2–3 days by reheating them in a static oven preheated to 350°F for 10–15 minutes.

Pollo alla Cacciatora
Chicken Cacciatora

Servings: 4 people

Ingredients

- 50 oz chicken (whole)
- 14 oz peeled tomatoes
- 1 onion
- 1 carrot
- 1 stalk celery
- 1 clove of garlic
- 0.6 cup red wine
- 1 tbsp extra virgin olive oil
- 1 sprig of rosemary
- A few leaves of chopped parsley
- Salt up to taste
- Black pepper to taste

DIRECTIONS:

1. To prepare the chicken cacciatore, start by cutting the vegetables. After cleaning the onion, peel the carrot and finally remove the topknot from the celery and wash it well. Finely chop everything.
2. Then move on to cleaning the chicken. Cut it into pieces separating the thighs, breast and wings. At this point, you'll have everything you need. Get to the stove.
3. In a large saucepan, heat the oil, just 1tbsp is enough because the skin of the chicken will release a lot of fat. Turn on the flame and let it heat for a few moments, then add the pieces of chicken, always starting from the skin side.
4. Leave to brown for about 10 minutes and then turn the pieces of chicken. When the chicken is well browned, add the chopped celery, carrot and onion and then the cleaned clove of garlic. Then salt, pepper and rosemary (you can leave the rosemary attached to the sprig so that you can remove it at the end of cooking, just wash it well), mix and leave to flavor for another 5 minutes.
5. Deglaze with the red wine and let the alcohol evaporate completely.
6. Remove the rosemary and the clove of garlic and then add the peeled chopped tomatoes. Stir everything together and cover with a lid, let it cook over gentle heat for 30–35 minutes.
7. Remember that if the pieces of chicken are very large, you will need to increase the cooking time a little more, and vice versa if they are smaller. In any case, the chicken is considered ready as soon as the meat separates from the bones.
8. At the end of cooking make sure it has just the right amount of salt and finally sprinkle with parsley. One last stir and the chicken cacciatore is ready, enjoy!

TIPS:

This dish is really tasty and the best part is the final "scarpetta".
My grandmother, when she prepared this recipe, also used the sauce to season the pasta (she often added a bit of tomato puree to the peeled tomatoes) and I must say that the taste was exceptional.
This recipe is typical Tuscan and is usually served with a sautéed side dish, such as peppers.
You can use the same recipe substituting chicken with rabbit, and also adding black olives to the sauce. Obviously, in case you choose to cook rabbit, pay attention to the cooking time which will be slightly shorter.

Peperonata
Peperonata

Servings: 4 people

Ingredients

- 35 oz red, yellow, and green peppers
- 14 oz red onions from Tropea
- 14 oz tomato puree
- 2 tbsp extra virgin olive oil
- 2 cloves of garlic
- Salt up to taste
- Black pepper to taste
- Fresh basil

DIRECTIONS:

1. To prepare the peperonata, wash and dry the peppers. Then slice them lengthwise, all around the core, remove the white filaments and seeds, and cut them into thin slices.
2. Also, clean and slice the onions and peel the garlic keeping it whole.
3. In a large saucepan pour the oil and garlic cloves. Heat and then add the onions. Stew the onions over medium-low heat for about 15 minutes, stirring occasionally.
4. When they are softened and have released their water, pour in the peppers. Season with salt and pepper, then stir and cover with a lid: cook the peppers for about 15 minutes more, over medium heat.
5. After this time the peppers will be softened, remove the garlic cloves and pour in the tomato puree, mix and cook for another 15 minutes with the lid on.
6. Once cooked, add the basil leaves and the peperonata will be ready to be enjoyed hot, warm or even cold and to accompany main courses of meat, fish or cheese!

TIPS:

This is a classic Peperonata recipe but you can have fun making this side dish into a unique dish.
You can add pieces of pork, sausage or chicken, 5 minutes after adding the peppers and continue with the preparation as per the recipe. This way you can serve a unique dish with a strong and tasty flavor!

Frittata di Cipolle
Onion Omelette

Servings: 2 people

Ingredients

- 4 eggs
- 1 golden onion
- Marjoram to taste
- 1 tbsp parmesan cheese
- 3 tbsp olive oil
- Salt to taste
- Pepper to taste
- 0.7 oz butter

DIRECTIONS:

1. To make the onion frittata, start by peeling and cutting the onion into thin slices of no more than 0.1 inches.
2. Let it season and brown in a pan with 3 tbsp of oil, about 5 minutes will be enough, stir occasionally to prevent sticking or burning.
3. In the meantime, beat the eggs not too long in a bowl. Add salt, pepper and parmesan cheese, add the chopped marjoram.
4. When the onions have cooled, add them to the eggs and place the mixture on the heat, in a non-stick pan in which you have melted a knob of butter. Distribute the onion well.
5. Reduce the heat and, after one or 2 minutes, when the eggs begin to set, shake the pan slightly to detach the omelette from the bottom and, using a flat plate or a lid, turn it over to cook it on the other side. Keep it on the heat as long as necessary, just a few minutes will be enough, especially if there are four eggs, as in this case.
6. Although the degree of cooking depends on taste, a very dry omelette is not recommended.

TIPS:

This dish can be served in these portions as a main course but, onion frittata, is a very versatile dish. You can cook it and cut it into small squares and serve it as an appetizer or even at brunch with friends or family.

Cotoletta alla Milanese
Milanese Schnitzel

Servings: 4 people

Ingredients

- 35 oz rib steak
- 4 large eggs
- 10 oz breadcrumbs
- 10 oz clarified butter
- Salt to taste

For a side dish of potatoes

- 17 oz potatoes
- 35 oz clarified butter
- 1 sprig of rosemary
- Salt to taste
- Black pepper to taste
- 1 clove of garlic

DIRECTIONS:

1. First of all, cut the veal loin into chops. To do this, carve the meat by running the knife between one bone and the other in order to obtain 4 ribs of about 8.75 oz each.
2. At this point scrape the bone with the tip of a knife so that it is completely clean. The hot butter will turn the handle of the bone clear.
3. Use a meat tenderizer to lightly pound the meat, in order to uniform the thickness without reducing it too much. Using the knife again, eliminate the superfluous nerves of the meat, which would make the cutlet shrink during cooking. Keep the meat aside and take care of the eggs.
4. Crack the eggs into a bowl and beat them with a whisk, without breaking them too much. If they are small, add another egg.
5. Instead, transfer the breadcrumbs to a large bowl.
6. Take the chops on the bone side and dip them first in the breadcrumbs, then dip them in the egg and again in the breadcrumbs, pressing well with your hands so that the breadcrumbs adhere well. Double-bread the ribs in the egg and in the breadcrumbs, pressing well but without flattening the meat too much. Repeat this operation for all the ribs.
7. Finally, with the non-cutting side of the knife, draw a sort of grid on the chops, first making horizontal lines and then vertical ones. Repeat the same thing for all the other cutlets and keep them aside without overlapping them and lay them on a sheet of baking paper.
8. Now take care of the potatoes. Wash the potatoes with some water and baking soda, then dry them well.
9. Then, with the help of a mandoline and a bowl full of water, cut into slices about 0.08 inches thick and gradually transfer them to the bowl full of water; in this way, they will release some starch and will not oxidize.
10. Pour some water into a saucepan, add a pinch of salt and bring it to a boil.
11. Then drain the potatoes and pour them into the pan with the boiling water. Cook for about 1 minute and a half then drain the potatoes again and let them cool slightly under cold water. By doing this pre-cooking the potatoes will cook for less time in the butter.
12. Dry the potatoes with a dish towel and in the meantime heat a fairly large pan with edges at least 1.5 inches high. Add the clarified butter and let it melt.
13. Add the potatoes, a lightly crushed clove of garlic, a sprig of rosemary and leave to brown on a high flame, tossing from time to time.
14. In the meantime, take another larger frying pan, which will be used for cooking the chops, and melt the butter. As soon as the butter is hot but not red-hot, place the chops in the pan, making sure that the ribbed side is in contact with the pan.
15. After about 4 minutes, the ribs will be nicely browned, so turn them over and with a spoon scoop out some of the cooking fat and sprinkle it on the rib bone; this way there won't be blood streaks but you'll get a clear bone.

16. The cutlets should cook for about another 4 minutes, this time depends in any case on the thickness of the meat, you should get pink meat inside.
17. Potatoes will have the same cooking time; when cooked season with salt and pepper.
18. When the ribs are ready, using tongs, transfer them to a plate with paper towels and, again using a sheet of paper, gently pat them dry to remove any excess fat.
19. At this point everything is ready, all you have to do is serve. Place the potatoes on the side of the plate, arrange the chop next to it and sprinkle with a little salt. Serve the Milanese veal chop piping hot and, if you wish, accompany it with a wedge of lemon that the guests can squeeze over to dilute the flavor of the fried meat.

TIPS:

You can ask the butcher directly to take the cutlets out of the whole piece of veal loin and clean the bone well. I often do this myself precisely to avoid this process.
If you prefer you can use extra virgin olive oil to cook the potatoes, but not to cook the cutlet. Instead of whole eggs, you can also use only the yolks; in this way, the breading will be more adherent to the meat, because during cooking the egg white tends to develop bubbles. Finally, I advise you not to salt the meat before breading it, otherwise, it will release liquids that will make the breading come off.

Frittata di Asparagi
Asparagus Omelette

Servings: 4 people

Ingredients

- 28 oz asparagus, not very large
- 6 medium eggs
- 1 leek
- Black pepper to taste
- 3 tbsp grana padano pdo
- 5 oz smoked scamorza
- 1 tbsp chives to chop
- 1.4 oz butter
- 3 tbsp extra virgin olive oil
- Salt up to taste

DIRECTIONS:

1. Start by washing the asparagus, remove the white and harder part of the stem. Then tie them together in bunches and boil them for about 15 minutes, standing them in salted water in a tall and narrow pot where only the tips can come out (they will cook with the steam). When they are cooked take them out and cut them into small pieces.
2. Clean the leek, removing the tough outer leaves, wash it and cut it into thin slices, which you will add to a pan in which you have melted the butter.
3. Wilt the leek, then season with salt and pepper and add the chopped asparagus; cook for a few minutes, until the asparagus stops losing its cooking water. At this point, season with salt, then turn off the heat and let the vegetables cool.
4. Beat the eggs in a bowl, add the ground pepper, grated cheese, warm vegetables, diced smoked provola and chives; mix the ingredients together well.
5. In a non-stick pan, pour the olive oil and heat it, then add the egg mixture and cook the omelette for 2–3 minutes over medium heat, then place a lid over the pan and lower the heat slightly, so the inside of the omelette will also cook evenly.
6. When the sides of the omelette start to turn golden brown, flip it over with the lid; brown the other side of the omelette and then slide it onto a serving plate.
7. Serve it hot by dividing it into wedges.

TIPS:

For the preparation of asparagus omelettes, I advise you to choose rather thin asparagus, or even wild asparagus (very thin and tasty), since after cooking they will be broken up and added to the egg mixture. Larger asparagus should be used as a side dish and not as a topping.

Finocchi Gratinati
Fennel Baked au Gratin

Servings: 4 people

Ingredients

- 4 large fennels
- 3 tbsp olive oil
- 3 tbsp grated parmesan cheese
- 4 oz breadcrumbs
- Salt and pepper to taste
- Garlic powder

DIRECTIONS:

1. To start, turn your oven on fan mode to 400°F and let it heat up.
2. Meanwhile, remove the fennel stalks, wash and dry them.
3. Cut each fennel in half and each half into thin slices, ½ inch maximum.
4. Take a large baking pan, cover it with baking paper and pour the fennel inside.
5. Add the olive oil, salt, pepper and garlic powder. Mix well and spread the fennel evenly inside the baking dish.
6. Finally, sprinkle with parmesan cheese and breadcrumbs.
7. Bake for 25 minutes. Once ready let them cool for 5 minutes and then serve them as a side dish with meat or fish. Enjoy your meal!

TIPS:

When they are cooked for 20 minutes, check that the fennel on the surface is browning. If they are not, set the oven to grill and leave to cook for a further 5–7 minutes.

Zucchine alla Scapece
Scapece Courgettes

Servings: 4 people

Ingredients

- 17 oz courgettes
- 2,5 oz extra virgin olive oil
- 1.4 oz white wine vinegar
- 2 cloves of garlic
- Mint to taste
- 7 oz fine salt
- Black pepper to taste
- Seed oil for frying to taste

DIRECTIONS:

1. To prepare the zucchini "alla scapece", start by peeling and washing the zucchini: cut them into rounds of about 0.12 inches, transfer them to a colander and add fine salt. Mix and cover with a dish towel: let the water drain for at least 30 minutes.
2. After 30 minutes, rinse the zucchini under running water, then dry them well on a dish towel.
3. Prepare the zucchini dressing: pour the olive oil into a bowl, add the white wine vinegar and salt. Mix everything with a fork, then add the previously washed and chopped mint, the peeled and chopped garlic cloves, pepper (you can also replace it with a pinch of ground chili) and mix everything together.
4. Heat the oil and fry a few zucchini at a time, it will take about 5 minutes and should brown.
5. In the meantime, prepare a shallow, wide oven dish in which to pour a first layer of dressing.
6. As you drain the zucchini, move them warm to the baking dish and create alternating layers with the dressing.
7. You can serve the zucchini alla scapece after they have cooled completely (at least a couple of hours) or even warm.

TIPS:

Zucchini alla scapece is one of the tastiest Neapolitan side dishes there is.
Zucchini alla scapece are excellent served as an appetizer with croutons or as a side dish, especially with fish dishes.

Melanzane a Funghetto
Mushroom Eggplants

Servings: 4 people

Ingredients

- 20 oz eggplants
- 20 oz ramato tomatoes
- 6 leaves of basil
- 1 clove of garlic
- Salt to taste
- Extra virgin olive oil to taste

DIRECTIONS:

1. To prepare the eggplants a funghetto, start by washing the eggplants under running water. Then remove the two ends with a knife, then cut the eggplants (from the long side) into 0.4-inch slices, divide them into strips, and cut them into 0.6-inch cubes.
2. Carefully wash the tomatoes, remove the stem and with a small knife remove the green part. Then cut the tomatoes into fairly thick slices and then into cubes.
3. Take a large frying pan and pour plenty of oil and when it is hot, add the eggplants to the pan: fry the them for about 10 minutes, turning them so that they brown evenly.
4. Using a slotted spoon, transfer the fried eggplant to a tray lined with paper towels to drain off excess oil.
5. In the same pan in which you fried the eggplant, brown a clove of garlic and as soon as it is browned remove it and add the diced tomatoes.
6. Break up the basil leaves with your hands and add them to the tomatoes. Cook for 5 minutes, then add the eggplants and let everything flavor for about 10 minutes over low heat, adding salt to taste.
7. Then turn off the heat and enjoy the eggplant mushrooms warm or cold, as a side dish or to flavor pasta!

TIPS:

Melanzane a funghetto is a classic and tasty vegetable side dish typical of Campania cuisine.
My grandmother used to use them to season pasta. She would cook the pasta and once it was ready, she would dip it in the pan with the eggplant mushrooms and then add the diced smoked provola cheese. I still remember the goodness of that pasta filante rich in flavor. Try dressing your pasta with this recipe, it will be delicious!

Polpettone
Baked Meatloaf

Servings: 6 people

Ingredients

- 22 oz ground beef (choose your favorite part of beef)
- 14 oz pork sausage
- 7 oz fresh bread
- 5 oz pecorino cheese to grate
- 7 oz whole milk
- 2 eggs
- 3 sprigs of thyme
- ½ tsp grated nutmeg
- Salt to taste
- Black pepper to taste
- Extra virgin olive oil to taste

DIRECTIONS:

1. First of all, remove the crust from the bread with a knife, cut it into cubes and put it into a bowl: you will need about 5 oz of breadcrumbs. Pour the milk into the bowl so that the bread absorbs it and softens.
2. Meanwhile, remove the casing from the sausage and crush it.
3. Pour the minced meat into another bowl, then add the sausage, the grated pecorino cheese, the bread soaked in milk and slightly squeezed, the whole eggs, the nutmeg, a few fresh thyme leaves, salt and pepper.
4. Knead with your hands to mix all the ingredients evenly.
5. Take a sheet of greaseproof paper onto which you are going to transfer the mixture and, using the sheet, form a cylinder, taking care to compact it well. Brush the meatloaf with olive oil.
6. Now preheat the oven to 300°F in static mode.
7. Take a large baking pan, place a sheet of baking paper inside, brush the sheet with olive oil, lay the meatloaf in the center of the pan and bake in a preheated oven at 350°F for about 80–90 minutes.
8. Once the cooking time is up, take the meatloaf out of the oven and serve piping hot together with a side dish of baked potatoes flavored with rosemary or even with a nice slice of aubergine parmigiana.

TIPS:

This is the recipe for the meatloaf that my mother used to prepare; my grandmother, however, enriched the recipe with smoked provola cheese.
When he spread the meat mixture on the baking paper, before creating the cylindrical shape, he would lay on the meat many small pieces of smoked provola cheese. Then he created the cylindrical shape and continued with the procedure I have indicated.
This way, once the meatloaf was cooked, when she prepared the portions, she would create these really tasty slices of stringy meatloaf.

Roastbeef alla Napoletana
Roastbeef Neapolitan Style

Servings: 6 people

Ingredients

- 35 oz rib roast
- 1 carrot
- 1 celery stalk
- 35 oz copper onions
- 1.25 cup extra virgin olive oil
- ½ tbsp lard
- 3–4 cherry tomatoes or some tomato paste (optional)
- 0.6 cup red wine
- Pepper

DIRECTIONS:

1. Start by cleaning and cutting the carrot and celery into small pieces.
2. Clean and chop the onions coarsely.
3. In a saucepan add ½ tbsp of lard and melt it along with the extra virgin oil.
4. Dip the celery and carrot into the pot and sauté.
5. Then add the meat and brown it slowly on all sides. When the meat is well browned on all sides, add a little pepper, pour in the wine and let it evaporate by raising the flame.
6. Meanwhile, chop the tomatoes and combine them, add a pinch of salt and cook for 10 minutes.
7. At this point remove the meat from the pan and move it to a tray covering it with silver paper and keep it in a warm place, even the oven off is fine.
8. Add the onions to the pot with the sauce, stir well, cover the pot with a lid and turn the heat down to low.
9. At this point, the Genovese must cook for at least 3 hours on a low flame (remember that, like all ragùs, the more it cooks, the better it is), the onions must be completely consumed and must become dark. If the sauce tends to dry out too much during cooking, add a little water.
10. Cut the roast beef into slices and top with the Genovese sauce.

Capretto al Forno con Patate
Baked Kid With Potatoes

Servings: 4 people

Ingredients

- 35 oz kid
- 26 oz white wine
- 1.6 cups water
- 3.5 oz white onions
- 6.3 oz carrots
- 6.3 oz celery
- 0.3 oz white wine vinegar
- 17 oz potatoes
- 1.7 oz extra virgin olive oil
- Salt up to taste
- Black pepper to taste
- 1 sprig of rosemary
- A few leaves of sage

- 3 bay leaves
- 2 juniper berries
- Black pepper in grains

DIRECTIONS:

1. Remove the fat from the meat, then cut it into pieces not too small.
2. Wash, peel and roughly chop the celery, carrot and onion that will be used to marinate the kid.
3. Transfer the vegetables to a large bowl along with the meat.
4. With a cotton kitchen string tie the herbs together and put them in the bowl, this way it will be easier to take them out after marinating.
5. Bathe everything with the wine and add the water to cover. Also, add the black peppercorns and juniper berries, wrap the bowl with cling film and leave the meat to marinate for 12 hours in the fridge.
6. After the time indicated has elapsed, take the marinated meat, remove the spices and herbs and drain off the preserving water with a colander. Keep the meat in the bowl and the herbs aside.
7. Wash the potatoes under running water to remove any earth residue from the skin and then with a mandoline knife form thin chips (without peeling them), pour them into a large baking dish and add the olive oil, salt and pepper and place on top the pieces of kid and herbs from the marinade; wet with a tbsp of vinegar and mix everything directly into the dish so that all the ingredients are flavored.
8. Bake the kid in a preheated static oven at 400°F for about 60 minutes, making sure to turn the kid while cooking.
9. Once ready, serve the roast kid with potatoes piping hot.

TIPS:

Grandma Lucia used to tell me that lamb is a symbol of sacrifice, in the Catholic religion, that's why it's always on the tables on Easter menus.
Whether you are a devotee of tradition or simply a foodie, this is the perfect recipe to prepare for a family Easter!

Gamberoni al Forno
Baked King Prawns

Servings: 4 people

Ingredients

- 12 king prawns
- 1.4 oz lemon juice
- 2.1 oz extra virgin olive oil
- Salt up to taste
- Black pepper to taste
- Parsley to taste

DIRECTIONS:

1. Start by cleaning the prawns: detach the legs from the prawns, remove the carapace, or the shell that covers the prawn, taking care not to remove either head or tail, to be left attached to the prawn as decoration.
2. Now remove the inner intestine: cut into the back of the shrimp with a small knife and remove the intestine of the shrimp, pulling it gently with the blade of the knife or with a toothpick.
3. Wash the sprig of parsley and chop it very finely.
4. Squeeze the lemon juice and prepare the citronette that will be used to flavor the baked prawns: put the parsley in a small bowl, pour the lemon juice, olive oil and salt and pepper. Emulsify the sauce well and keep it aside.
5. Take a rectangular oven dish, lay the cleaned prawns next to each other, and flavor them with the citronette poured directly over the crustaceans.
6. Cover the shrimp with a sheet of baking paper, which will serve to keep the moisture inside so they stay tender.
7. Bake in a static oven preheated to 400°F for 10–12 minutes.
8. When cooked, take the baked prawns out of the oven and serve piping hot, cover with a spoonful of the cooking sauce and serve with a fresh side dish, such as a fennel and orange salad or a zucchini scapece.

Alici Fritte
Fried Anchovies

Servings: 4 people

Ingredients

- 17 oz anchovies
- 7 oz breadcrumbs
- 7 oz flour
- 2 eggs
- Peanut seed oil to taste
- Salt and pepper

DIRECTIONS:

1. Take the anchovies and remove the heads and bones.
2. Open all the anchovies well and rinse them under running water. Then arrange them on a plate and set them aside.
3. Prepare three different bowls: one with flour, one with the 2 eggs (beaten with a fork) and one with the breadcrumbs.
4. Take each anchovy by the tail and dip it first in the flour (shake off the excess flour), then dip it in the beaten eggs and finally in the breadcrumbs, pressing well with your hands so that the breadcrumbs stick perfectly to the whole surface of the anchovies.
5. Heat plenty of peanut oil in a narrow, high-sided pan to 300°F.
6. Dip 2 or 3 anchovies at a time so as not to lower the temperature of the oil too much.
7. Fry the anchovies for a few minutes and when they are golden brown, place them on a sheet of blotting paper.
8. Serve the fried anchovies piping hot with a sprinkle of salt and pepper.

TIPS:

This recipe is a delight! I remember as a child hiding under the table while my grandmother fried anchovies; as soon as they were ready, I would sneak out and steal one. I really liked them hot.
I recommend serving them with a simple salad dressed in olive oil, lemon and salt.

Gateau di Patate
Potato Gateau

Servings: 6 people

Ingredients

- 17 oz yellow-fleshed potatoes
- 3.5 oz milk cream
- 1.7 oz salami
- 1,7 oz cooked ham
- 2 tbsp Parmigiano Reggiano DOP (aged 24 months)
- 2 eggs
- Extra virgin olive oil to taste
- Black pepper to taste
- Salt up to taste

To season the top of the gateau

- Extra virgin olive oil to taste
- 0,7 oz breadcrumbs
- 1 oz parmesan cheese pdo

DIRECTIONS:

1. Start by boiling the potatoes. Rinse them well and pour them into a large pot, covering them completely with plenty of cold water. Put the pot on the stove and let them boil for about 30–40 minutes. Test them with a fork to make sure they are actually cooked: if it easily reaches the center of the potatoes, they are ready.
2. Drain the potatoes and peel them while they're still hot, helping yourself with a small knife so you don't burn yourself.
3. After peeling them, mash them immediately in a bowl: when the potatoes are hot, they are easier to unravel and will not present lumps.
4. In the meantime, cut the mozzarella into cubes and place it in a colander to squeeze it, so that it will drain the excess whey.
5. Cut the salami into cubes of about 0.4 inches; do the same with a slice of cooked ham.
6. At this point, take the freshly mashed potatoes and add the eggs, a sprinkling of pepper, salt, a little oil and grated Parmesan cheese.
7. Mix the ingredients together and when the mixture is well blended, you can add the diced ham and salami.
8. Then pour the drained mozzarella into the bowl and mix all the ingredients together.
9. Now grease an 8 x 8 inch square baking dish and sprinkle with the breadcrumbs. Shake the pan to make sure the breadcrumbs are spread all over the surface.
10. Then pour the mixture, using a spatula to level it.
11. Sprinkle the surface with the breadcrumbs and Parmesan cheese, season again with a drizzle of oil and bake in a static oven preheated to 350°F for about 30 minutes.
12. Once cooked, leave the gateau to rest for about 15 minutes before serving.

TIPS:

Grandma Lucia used to say that in the Gateau "you put whatever you can find", so indulge yourself by using cold meats and cheeses of your choice to stuff the Gateau, such as mortadella, bacon, etc.
If the potatoes you used are too floury, you can dilute the mixture with a little milk, as the true Neapolitan tradition requires.

Parmigiana di Patate
Parmigiana of Potatoes

Servings: 6 people

Ingredients for an 11x7 inch baking pan

- 35 oz of potatoes
- 5,6 oz cooked ham
- 12 oz sweet provolone
- 3.5 oz Grana Padano DOP (to grate)
- Salt up to taste
- Black pepper to taste

For the béchamel

- 2 cups whole milk
- 1.7 oz butter
- 0.9 oz flour
- Nutmeg to taste
- Black pepper to taste
- 1 pinch fine salt

DIRECTIONS:

1. Start with the béchamel sauce. In a saucepan pour the butter and melt it, then add the sifted flour and stir to avoid creating lumps. Add the hot milk and continue stirring to thicken the mixture over low heat. Flavor the béchamel with grated nutmeg and add a pinch of salt and pepper. Continue to mix with the whisk until the béchamel has reached a creamy consistency, turn off the heat and let it cool in a bowl covered with plastic wrap that will touch the surface of the béchamel.
2. Peel the potatoes and blanch them for 10 minutes in water to soften them slightly, they should not flake but remain intact, the cooking time may vary depending on the size of the potatoes.
3. Drain and let them cool slightly, then cut them into slices about 0.2 inches thick.
4. Cut the provolone into slices about 0.2 inches thick.
5. Take the oven dish, spread a layer of béchamel sauce on the bottom, using the back of a spoon.
6. Lay half of the potato slices on top of each other.
7. Season with salt and pepper and then spread another layer of béchamel sauce on top, then lay half of the provolone slices on top.
8. Now cover everything with half of the cooked ham.
9. Start creating another layer: spread the béchamel sauce, sprinkle with grated cheese and lay the remaining potato slices on top.
10. Cover everything with more béchamel sauce, then distribute the remaining slices of cooked ham, continue again with the béchamel sauce and the remaining provolone and finally sprinkle the surface with grated cheese.
11. Bake for 40–45 minutes in a static oven preheated to 350ºF.
12. After the necessary time, you can check the cooking by inserting a toothpick: if you can easily pierce the potatoes, the potato parmigiana is ready!

TIPS:

Again, you can use any meats and cheeses you prefer or have on hand to stuff the potato parmigiana. I also add a personal touch. On the surface, I sprinkle hazelnut crumbs; when the crust is created by the béchamel on the surface, the hazelnuts become crunchy and fragrant. Try it yourself!

Salmone Marinato
Marinated Salmon

Servings: 4 people

Ingredients

- 1 salmon fillet (fresh)
- White wine vinegar
- Pink pepper in grains to taste
- 2 cloves of garlic
- Hot pepper (optional) to taste
- 3 tbsp lemon juice
- Salt to taste
- A tuft fresh parsley

DIRECTIONS:

1. Wash the fresh fish. In case you are using a whole salmon, remove the head and guts and wash the fish well under running water.
2. Freeze fresh fish before marinating it, this will also ensure food safety because freezing kills any bacteria present in raw fish.
3. Take the salmon out of the freezer and while it's still semi frozen slice it into thin slices. Fresh fish is more difficult to slice, while semi-frozen fish can be sliced thinly and perfectly.
4. Place the salmon slices in a bowl and season with fine salt, cover completely with the white wine vinegar and lemon juice.
5. Let it rest for about 4–5 hours.
6. After the resting time has elapsed, drain the salmon and rinse under running water to remove excess vinegar.
7. Place the salmon slices in a bowl, add the extra virgin olive oil, pink peppercorns, chili pepper to taste, chopped fresh parsley and add more fine salt if necessary.
8. Serve the marinated salmon as an appetizer or make delicious bruschetta with slices of toasted bread and place a slice of marinated salmon on top of each one.

TIPS:

With the same procedure used for salmon you can also prepare marinated swordfish or anchovies, sea bream fillet and so on. With this procedure, in practice, you can marinate any type of fresh fish to your liking.

Calamari Fritti
Fried Calamari

Servings: 4 people

Ingredients

- 31 oz calamari
- 7 oz flour
- Salt up to taste

For frying

- 4 cups peanut seed oil

DIRECTIONS:

1. Start by cleaning the squid: rinse under plenty of fresh running water, then with your hands gently remove the head from the mantle. Once the head is extracted, always with your hands, look for the transparent cartilage pen that is in the mantle and extract it gently.
2. Run the squid under running water again, wash it thoroughly and use your hands to extract the innards from the shell.
3. Remove the outer skin: cut the end of the mantle with a small knife, just enough to take a strip of skin, and pull the covering completely off with your hands or with the help of a small knife. Remove the fins.
4. Cut the mantle into rings 0.2 inches thick or alternatively you can cut thin strips: open the mantle like a book, and with a knife cut the end in half and cut strips.
5. Take the tentacles and remove the central tooth. Put everything in a colander to remove excess water.
6. Now take care of the breadcrumbs: on a tray distribute the flour, then arrange the squid rings, mixing them so that the breadcrumbs adhere well on all sides.
7. Pass them through a colander so they lose excess flour.
8. Place a large pot with the frying oil on the stove, make sure the temperature reaches 325°F with the help of a kitchen thermometer.
9. Now fry the breaded rings a few at a time for 3–4 minutes, until golden brown and crispy.
10. Drain them with a skimmer and place them on a tray lined with paper towels to drain excess oil.
11. Adjust the salt to taste and serve the fried squid hot.

TIPS:

For a touch of freshness, I suggest you serve a wedge of lemon with the squid, to squeeze over the fried food.

Peperoni Ripieni al Forno

Peppers Stuffed With Meat and Sausage

Servings: 4 people

Ingredients

- 4 large peppers

For the stuffing

- 10 oz ground veal
- 5 oz sausage
- 3.5 oz stale bread crumbs
- 1.7 oz Grana Padano DOP for grating
- 7 oz provolone or smoked provolone cheese
- 5 oz whole milk
- 2 eggs
- 0,4 oz parsley to chop
- Salt up to taste
- Black pepper to taste

To grate

- 0.7 oz Grana Padano DOP for grating
- 0.7 oz provolone cheese for grating
- Basil

DIRECTIONS:

1. First cut the stale bread into cubes, place it in a bowl and cover with milk. Press the bread lightly so that it absorbs the milk well.
2. Move on to the peppers: wash and dry them.
3. Remove the upper cap and take out the filaments and internal seeds. Take back the capsules, cut off the part around the stalk, so as to eliminate it and cut the pieces of pepper into fairly small cubes.
4. Remove the casing from the sausage and pour it into a large bowl, where you will also add the ground meat.
5. Squeeze the bread softened in milk well. Add it to the meat and knead well.
6. Add the provolone cut into very small pieces and the grated Grana cheese; mix with your hands.
7. Pour in the 2 whole eggs, and the diced peppers and knead again.
8. Add the salt, pepper and chopped parsley. Mix everything together well until smooth.
9. Take the peppers you have left whole, place them inside an oven dish and fill to the brim with the meat and sausage filling. Press with the back of a spoon to compact the filling.
10. Add a drizzle of oil and bake in a static oven preheated to 350°F for 40 minutes on the middle rack.
11. After 40 minutes, take the peppers out of the oven, sprinkle with grated Grana cheese and a few more cubes of provolone. Return to the oven, in grill mode at 470°F for 3–4 minutes.
12. When the cheese has melted you can take them out of the oven, add some basil leaves and serve the stuffed peppers after letting them rest for 5 minutes.

TIPS:

This recipe is very versatile; you can create the filling to your liking. I often cook also the vegetarian version where the filling is composed of: rice, onions, peas, carrots, cherry tomatoes and provolone cheese. To prepare this version all you need to do is cook the rice in white (drain it at least 3–4 minutes before it finishes cooking); on the side, sauté the chopped onions, chopped carrot, peas and diced cherry tomatoes in a pan with a little olive oil. Sauté for 10 minutes and add everything to the rice; add a tbsp of olive oil and mix everything together. Add the diced provolone and mix again. Now fill the peppers and continue with the same procedure as the recipe above.

Scaloppina al Limone
Escalopes With Lemon

Servings: 4 people

Ingredients

- 8 slices veal (about 15–16 oz)
- 1.7 oz lemon juice
- Salt up to taste
- Black pepper to taste

To flour and bake

- Flour to taste
- 1.4 oz butter

DIRECTIONS:

1. First of all beat the veal slices with the help of a meat tenderizer, covering them with baking paper so as not to break the fibers: beat with a firm but delicate hand, in this way the tissues will soften without tearing the flesh (if you do not have a meat tenderizer you can use the bottom of a glass).
2. In a dish pour the flour and flour the veal slices and remove the excess flour by shaking them.
3. Melt the butter in a large frying pan over low heat, then add the slices of meat, turn up the heat slightly and brown for a couple of minutes first on one side and then on the other. Season with salt and pepper.
4. At this point, lower the flame again and deglaze with the lemon juice.
5. Cook over gentle heat for a couple of minutes, just long enough for the sauce to set. Turn off the heat and serve your fragrant lemon escalopes immediately.

TIPS:

Once served, season the slices with a little thyme and accompany the escalopes with a side dish such as baked potatoes or artichokes au gratin.

Orata all'Acqua Pazza
Bream in Acqua Pazza

Servings: 4 people

Ingredients

- 31 oz bream (1 or 2 depending on weight)
- 10.5 oz cherry tomatoes
- A sprig parsley
- ¾ cloves of garlic
- 2 tbsp extra virgin olive oil
- Salt to taste
- Pepper to taste
- 0.3 cup water
- 0.3 cup white wine

DIRECTIONS:

1. Start by cleaning the sea bream. Scale and remove all the fins from the sea bream. Make a cut on the belly and gut the fish. Rinse the sea bream under fresh running water making sure you have cleaned the inside of the fish thoroughly.
2. Put a pinch of salt, a peeled clove of garlic and a couple of parsley leaves inside the belly.
3. Take an oven dish and sprinkle the bottom with extra virgin olive oil, then lay the sea breams.
4. Cut the cherry tomatoes into wedges or cubes and add them to the oven dish together with the remaining 2 cloves of garlic cut into slices, the leafy parsley, salt and pepper, water and white wine; the liquids should not cover the sea bream completely but remain less than half the height of the fish.
5. Bake in a preheated oven at 425°F for about 20–25 minutes.
6. When the gilthead bream all'acqua pazza is cooked, remove the oven dish from the oven, place the gilthead bream on a plate, remove the skin and divide it into fillets, eliminating all the bones (the large central one and the side ones) and the head.
7. Once you have obtained the fillets, place them in a serving dish drizzling them with the cooking juices and serve immediately.

Mozzarella in Carrozza
Mozzarella in a Wagon

Servings: 24 pieces

Ingredients

- 12 slices white bread loaf (approx. 21 oz)
- 17 oz buffalo mozzarella preferably the day before
- Salt up to taste
- 5 large eggs
- 3.5 oz flour
- 11 oz breadcrumbs

For frying

- 4 cups sunflower seed oil

DIRECTIONS:

1. Cut the buffalo mozzarella into slices 0,4 inches thick. Arrange them by hand on a tray lined with paper towels and cover them with more paper towels. Press gently with your hands, to blot the mozzarella and remove excess water. If necessary, change the sheets of paper towels until completely dry.
2. At this point, proceed to stuff the bread. Arrange 6 slices of bread on a cutting board, place the slices of mozzarella on top, so as to cover the entire surface, but without spilling it, add a pinch of salt and cover with another slice of bread. Press with your hands to compact everything. Continue in this way for all the other slices until you have finished the mozzarella.
3. Then trim the stuffed bread slices using a knife, so that the outer crust is removed.
4. Now move on to the breadcrumbs. Crack the eggs into a dish and beat them with a whisk for a few minutes.
5. Then in 2 other baking dishes, place the breadcrumbs in one and the sifted flour in the other.
6. At this point pass each piece of bread stuffed first in the flour and then in the egg, so as to cover them entirely. Then pass them on a plate for a few seconds, so as to remove the excess egg and avoid lumps when you pass them into the breadcrumbs. Then pass them in the breadcrumbs.
7. Transfer to a cutting board and use the blade of a knife to lightly press the edges and the surface in order to even out the breadcrumbs and get a more precise shape. If necessary, dip again in the breadcrumbs and press again with the knife blade. Continue in this way for all the other pieces and gradually transfer them onto a tray lined with greaseproof paper. Put in the fridge for about 30 minutes.
8. After the mozzarellas in Carrozza have firmed up, you can move on to the second breading, first dip them in the egg, then in the saucer to remove the excess and finally in the breadcrumbs. As you did before, transfer the pieces of mozzarella in Carrozza on a cutting board and with the blade of a knife uniform the breadcrumbs. Continue in this way for all the other slices, placing them on a tray lined with greaseproof paper. Place in the fridge to firm up for another 30 minutes.
9. Pour the seed oil into a pan and bring it to a temperature of 350°F maximum.
10. Dip a few pieces at a time and cook the mozzarella in Carrozza for 1–2 minutes, turning them occasionally with a skimmer.
11. When they are golden brown, remove them from the oil with a slotted spoon and transfer them to a tray lined with paper towels to remove excess oil.
12. Serve the mozzarella in Carrozza still hot so it will be nice and stringy.

TIPS:

To prepare the mozzarella in Carrozza I recommend using a non-fresh mozzarella, so it will be drier. In this way, it will not risk coming out during cooking.
In order to make sure that the breadcrumbs stick well to the bread and do not develop moisture inside, it is important to place them in the refrigerator after each loaf.
Be very careful when frying. If the oil is too hot the mozzarella in Carrozza will be too colored on the outside, but inside it will not be stringy.

Baccalà in Umido con Polenta
Codfish Stew With Polenta

Servings: 4 people

Ingredients

- 28 oz cod fillet already desalted
- 2 small white or golden onions
- 12.3 oz peeled tomatoes
- 1 hot pepper
- 3 anchovy fillets in oil
- 4 tbsp extra virgin olive oil
- 1 cup vegetable bouillon
- Salt and pepper to taste
- 0.3 cup dry white wine
- Chopped parsley to taste
- 3 garlic cloves

For the polenta

- 17 oz cornmeal
- 8 cups water
- 1.5 tbsp extra virgin olive oil
- 1 tbsp coarse salt

DIRECTIONS:

1. Peel and thinly slice the onion and peel the garlic. Chop the chili pepper with a knife and add everything to a large pan with the oil already hot.
2. Fry for a few minutes over low heat then add the anchovy fillets, stir and add the peeled tomatoes crushed with a fork.
3. Deglaze with the white wine, then add a pinch of salt and pepper and finally pour the boiling broth (you can prepare the same light broth I recommended in the previous recipes), cover with a lid and, when it boils, lower the heat to a minimum. Let it cook for about 15 minutes.
4. In the meantime, place a thick-bottomed steel pot on the stove, pour in the 4 cups of water.
5. Cut the washed cod fillet into slices and pat dry with kitchen paper. Add the slices to the sauce and leave to cook for another 20 minutes.
6. Halfway through cooking time gently turn the fish with the help of a spatula, add the chopped parsley and finally close the pan with the lid, turn off the flame and leave the cod covered.
7. When the water is about to come to a boil add the coarse salt, then pour in the flour by sprinkling, stirring with a wooden spoon, keep cooking at a high temperature stirring quickly.
8. Add also the olive oil that will serve to avoid the formation of lumps. Keep stirring and wait for it to come to the boil, then lower the heat to the minimum and continue cooking for 50 minutes over a gentle heat, stirring continuously, taking care not to let the polenta stick to the bottom.
9. When the 50 minutes have elapsed, the polenta is ready; turn up the heat so that it comes off the pan well.
10. Meanwhile, turn the heat back on under the pan of stewed cod.
11. Now invert the polenta pan onto a round cutting board a little larger than the diameter of the pan to unmold it.
12. At this point, lay the stewed codfish on the polenta and serve it hot.

TIPS:

This winter dish is really tasty and full-bodied.
I always serve it in the way I have described as my grandmother used to do, that is a single large portion in the middle of the table so that the guests can serve themselves. If you prefer you can create portions on the plate without turning the polenta upside down on the cutting board but pouring it into individual plates with a large spoon and then add the portion of stewed salt cod.

Fiori di Zucca Ripieni
Battered Pumpkin Flowers

Servings: 4 people

Ingredients

- 15 pumpkin flowers
- Salt up to taste
- Peanut seed oil for frying to taste

For the stuffing

- 8.8 oz ricotta cheese
- 7 oz cooked ham one large slice
- Salt and pepper to taste

For the batter

- 0.9 cup warm mineral water
- 5.3 oz flour
- 0.5 oz fresh brewer's yeast
- 0.2 oz fine salt
- 0.2 oz sugar

DIRECTIONS:

1. Start by making the batter. First dissolve the fresh yeast, crumbled by hand, with a little water at room temperature. Emulsify with a whisk.
2. In another bowl pour the flour, add the remaining room temperature water and mix with a whisk until smooth and without lumps; then add the brewer's yeast just dissolved in the water, continuing to whisk.
3. Add the sugar and salt, mix again to combine the ingredients and cover with plastic wrap. Let stand for about 30 minutes at room temperature.
4. Prepare the filling: take the ricotta, put it in a colander and let it drain.
5. Take a bowl and pour in the ricotta, salt, pepper and diced cooked ham. Mix everything with a fork until you get a smooth cream.
6. Now take care of the pumpkin flowers: delicately detach the stem. Then, always with your hands, pull away both the external pistils and the internal bud; repeat the same operation for all of them.
7. Now take one by one, gently open it with your hands and, with a spoon or a sac-a´ poche, fill it with a portion of ricotta filling.
8. Once the 30 minutes have passed, the classic batter will well rise, so take care of the frying.
9. Pour the oil into a saucepan and bring it to a temperature of 350°F maximum (use a kitchen thermometer to do this).
10. Once the oil has almost reached the indicated temperature, dip the flowers in the batter and, using pincers, turn them over so that they are completely covered. Then extract each flower from the batter, letting the excess drip and making sure that the tip is well sealed by the batter so that during frying the filling does not come out of the flower.
11. Dip a few pieces at a time in hot oil so as not to lower the temperature of the oil too much. When they are well browned, turn them over and continue cooking on the other side.
12. Using a slotted spoon, remove the courgette flowers from the oil and place them on a sheet of absorbent paper. Season with a pinch of salt and serve the zucchini flowers in batter warm.

TIPS:

Another very tasty filling is also that of burrata cheese and sun-dried tomatoes in oil; you can also prepare zucchini flowers in batter without filling.

Montanarine
Neapolitan Mountaineers

Servings: 30 pieces

For the dough of the Neapolitan Montanare

- 10.5 oz flour
- O.75 cup water
- ½ tsp dry brewer's yeast
- 1 tsp sugar
- 0.28 oz salt
- 1 tbsp extra virgin olive oil

To season the Neapolitan Montanare

- 1 garlic
- 1 tbsp extra virgin olive oil
- 7 oz tomato sauce
- 1 pinch of salt
- 0.7 oz Grana Padano DOP grated
- Basil to taste

DIRECTIONS:

1. First sift the flour, add ½ tsp of dry brewer's yeast and 1 tsp of sugar, and stir to mix the ingredients.
2. Knead by slowly pouring in the water until it is completely absorbed by the dough.
3. After adding all the water to the flour, pour in 1 tbsp of oil and continue kneading.
4. As the last ingredient add the salt, the dough will be well homogeneous and elastic.
5. Pour it on the floured pastry board and knead for 30 seconds more, give the dough a round shape.
6. Place the Neapolitan Montanare dough in an oiled bowl, cover with plastic wrap and let rise until doubled in size. With this dose of yeast, you will need about 3 hours.
7. In the meantime prepare the sauce: heat 1 tbsp of oil in a pan with a clove of garlic, pour in the tomato sauce and add a pinch of salt. Cook for about 10 minutes until the sauce becomes thick. Let it cool.
8. When the dough has doubled in size, roll out the dough on a floured surface and cut out rounds with a pastry cutter or simply with a glass.
9. Put plenty of oil in a frying pan and bring it to about 350° F, crush the "Montanare" in the middle to give the hollow in which the seasoning will be put and fry them.
10. Turn them over to brown them on both sides. Once golden brown, drain them with a slotted spoon and place them on a sheet of absorbent paper towels, then place them on a serving plate.
11. Complete by pouring a spoonful of hot tomato sauce, a sprinkling of grated Grana Padano cheese and a leaf of basil.
12. Serve the Montanare still warm!

TIPS:

This recipe is suitable as an appetizer or even as a dish for brunch or an aperitif with friends. I remember that my grandmother used to prepare them when we watched the World Cup together. I have to say that even if I was never a big fan, I remember those moments together with great happiness and even now, during the World Cup, the whole family gets together and I prepare Montanare with my mom!

Melanzane a Scarpone
Scarpone Aubergines

Servings: 4 people

Ingredients

- 4 small aubergines
- 7 oz cherry tomatoes
- 1.7 oz green and black olives
- 0.17 oz smoked scamorza cheese
- 0.17 oz grated parmesan cheese
- 1 tbsp pickled capers
- Breadcrumbs to taste
- Basil to taste
- Extra virgin olive oil to taste
- Salt to taste

For frying

- Seed oil

DIRECTIONS:

1. Wash the aubergines and cut them in half lengthwise. Cut with a knife the flesh of the aubergine and extract it with the help of a spoon.
2. Prepare a pan with plenty of seed oil and bring it to 350°F.
3. Drain the aubergine on a sheet of paper towels, turning the hollowed-out part toward the paper towel.
4. Dice the aubergine flesh and fry it in seed oil.
5. Fry the aubergine halves, too.
6. If you want you can bake them in the oven by proceeding the same way but baking the diced aubergine flesh and the drained aubergine halves in a preheated 400°F oven for 20 minutes.
7. Put in a bowl the tomatoes washed and cut into small pieces and well drained of excess water, the pieces of aubergine flesh, diced scamorza cheese, pitted green and black olives, capers, fresh basil chopped by hand, salt and extra virgin olive oil and mix well to mix everything.
8. Fill the fried (or baked) aubergine halves with the filling, sprinkle the surface with breadcrumbs and grated parmesan cheese.
9. Bake the aubergine boot in a preheated 400°F oven for 10 minutes so that the scamorza melts and a crispy crust forms on the surface.
10. Pop the aubergine in the oven and let them cool. You can serve them either hot or cold, they will still be great.

TIPS:

You can create a different stuffing according to your tastes; for example, I often stuff them with a sauce made with oil, onion, minced beef and tomato puree. I add the sauce to the pieces of aubergine flesh, stuff the eggplant and top with a few pieces of smoked provolone and breadcrumbs. A real delicacy!

Peperoncini Verdi con Pomodoro
Green Chillies With Tomato

Servings: 4 people

Ingredients

- 35 oz green chilies
- 1.7 oz cherry tomatoes
- Peanut seed oil to taste
- Salt up to taste
- Basil

DIRECTIONS:

1. Rinse the chilies under water and then dry them perfectly with a clean tea towel. Then move to the stove.
2. In a large frying pan pour the seed oil until it covers the base of the pan. When the oil is hot, pour in the chilies in several batches, almost until the pan is full, and let them cook over medium-high heat, being careful of oil splashes.
3. Turn the green chilies occasionally to cook evenly - they will take a few minutes.
4. As the peppers are cooked, scoop them out with a slotted spoon and put them to drain in a bowl with paper towels.
5. In the meantime, wash, dry and cut the cherry tomatoes into four pieces and place them in a bowl.
6. As soon as all the green chilies are cooked, set them aside and, in the frying pan where you fried them, remove the oil leaving just a trickle.
7. Add the cherry tomatoes to the pan. Cooking them in the same oil will allow the cherry tomatoes to season even more. Let them cook for 10 minutes on a medium flame, add salt to taste and finally plunge the chilies into the pan, letting them flavor in the sauce for a few minutes. Turn off the heat, add the basil leaves washed and chopped with your hands and mix.
8. All you have left to do is enjoy your tomato green chilies! Use them as a side dish to a nice steak, too!

TIPS:

This recipe is also great for dressing pasta, such as pennette or even spaghetti, which you will sprinkle with grated Parmesan cheese.

Piadina Romagnola
Piadina Romagnola

Servings: 6 people

Ingredients

- 17.5 oz Flour 00
- 4.5 oz Lard
- 6 oz Water at room temperature
- 0.5 oz Fine salt
- 1.5 tsp. baking soda

DIRECTIONS:

1. Prepare the dough by combining the flour, salt, lard and baking soda in a bowl.
2. Knead and add the water in 3 times, then transfer the mixture to a work surface and continue working until a smooth dough is obtained. Form into a ball, wrap it in a food bag and let it rest for 30 minutes.
3. After the resting time has elapsed, remove the dough from the bag and form a sausage, then divide it into 6 equal portions. Give each one the shape of a ball by kneading it for about 30 seconds so that it becomes smooth and even, then wrap the 6 balls again with a food bag and let them rest for another 30 minutes.
4. After the second resting time has elapsed, lightly flour the work surface and roll out the balls with a rolling pin to a thickness of 0.1 inch. Heat a griddle well and in the meantime roll out the piadinas further, then cup them with an 8.5-inch-diameter ramekin (or with the help of a knife and a baking pan of the same size, lay the pan over the dough and trim the edges, making them round).
5. Now cook the piadinas on one side for 2 minutes, rotating them over themselves continuously with one hand to ensure even cooking, then turn them over and cook them for 2 minutes on the other side as well, until they are lightly browned. Once cooked, stack the piadinas on top of each other and stuff them while still hot.

TIPS:

If you want to get a softer piadina, you can replace part of the water dose with milk. Instead for a vegetarian version, you can use 2.8 oz of extra virgin olive oil instead of lard.

To stuff the piadina you can use sliced meats or a meat (Chicken, cooked or raw ham, mortadella, salami, etc.), or even tofu for a vegetarian version, seasoned grilled vegetables (zucchini, eggplant, etc.) or a rich salad and accompany it with a sauce (yogurt sauce, mustard, guacamole, tzatziki, hummus, etc.). In any case, let taste guide you in stuffing them; piadina is always a tasty and quick dish to prepare.

DESSERTS

Pastiera Napoletana
Neapolitan Pastiera

Servings: 8 people

**For the shortcrust pastry
(for an 8-inch round mold)**

- 8.81 oz flour
- 1.76 oz lard
- 1.76 oz butter
- 2.82 oz sugar
- 0.70 oz wildflower honey
- 1 medium egg
- 1,4 oz whole milk
- ½ lemon peel
- ½ orange peel
- 1 pinch fine salt

**For the cream
of wheat**

- 7 oz cooked wheat
- 2.82 oz whole milk
- 0.88 oz butter
- Lemon peel to taste
- Orange peel to taste
- 1 pinch fine salt

**For the rest of
the stuffing**

- 7 oz sheep's
  milk ricotta
- 6.35 oz sugar
- 1.76 oz candied
  citron
- 0,70 multi-flower
  honey
- 2 whole eggs
- 1 egg yolk
- Orange blossom
  water to taste
- 0.70 whole milk
- Orange peel to taste
- Lemon peel to taste

To garnish

- Icing sugar to taste

DIRECTIONS:

1. To prepare the pastiera, start with the shortcrust pastry. Sieve the flour on the work surface, add a pinch of salt. Form a well, with a central hole deep enough to see the work surface in the center.
2. In the center add the chopped butter, lard and sugar. Work the fat and sugar by hand to absorb them.
3. While continuing to stir, add the honey, then the egg and milk. Then grate the orange and lemon zest.
4. Keep working the ingredients in the center, you will get a sort of soft batter. Then slowly start to take the flour from the sides and knead the dough. You will have to get a ball, to make it more homogeneous you can lightly dust the work surface with a little flour. Knead the dough again to make it completely smooth and homogeneous. Cover with clingfilm and leave to rest in the fridge for 1 hour.
5. Move on to cooking the wheat. In a saucepan pour the pre-cooked wheat, add a pinch of salt. Mash the wheat a little to make it uniform and wet with the milk.
6. Add the butter. Add a small piece of orange and lemon zest without grating them so they can be removed when cooked. Stir everything together. Bring to a simmer, it will take a few minutes: use a fork to mash the grain while it cooks and stir constantly.
7. When it's about to boil, turn it off and transfer the mixture to a shallow, wide dish to cool (if you don't like to hear the grain in chunks, at this point you can take an immersion blender and blend the mixture so that the grain is totally reduced, before blending remove the citrus peels).
8. In a separate bowl sift the ricotta and add the sugar. Mix until smooth and refrigerate for 1 hour or so.
9. After the time has elapsed, recover the wheat mixture, now cold, remove the citrus peels and transfer everything into a large bowl. Add the diced candied citron and mix briefly.
10. Retrieve the bowl with the ricotta and sugar, add the honey, stir and add it to the wheat mixture, always stirring to incorporate.
11. In another bowl add the 2 eggs and yolk and pour in the orange blossom water.
12. Add milk, grate some lemon and orange zest, and mix well.
13. Combine this mixture with the ricotta and wheat cream, continuing to mix. And the filling is ready.

14. Take the shortcrust pastry and divide it into two parts, one larger than the other. Roll out the larger part with a rolling pin on a lightly floured surface. You will need to get to a thickness of about 0,12 inches. Then roll the dough on the rolling pin.
15. Roll out the pastry in the pie tin. Make the pastry stick well to the bottom and the edges, then remove the excess pastry and trim the edges with the help of a small knife. Make small holes in the base of the pastry with a fork.
16. Transfer the cream to the inside, gently banging the pan on the top to remove any air bubbles.
17. Roll out with a rolling pin on a lightly floured surface the leftover dough and make 7 strips 0.4–0.7 inches thick at most. Place the first 4 up to beyond the edge of the pastiera, crosswise. Then over the other 3 to create the lattice, always reaching the edge of the pie pan. Remove any excess pastry.
18. The pastiera at this point is ready to bake in a static oven preheated to 350°F, for about 50–55 minutes on the lowest rack of the oven but not directly on the bottom.
19. Take the pastiera out of the oven and when it has cooled completely you can turn it out of the mould (or serve it directly in the pan), dusting it with a little icing sugar before serving.

TIPS:

Grandma used to tell me that, according to Neapolitan tradition, the 7 strips of short pastry that cover the pastiera represent the plan of the ancient city of Neapolis, which is the historical center of Naples today. The strips, therefore, represent the three Decumani and the four Cardini of the ancient Greek city.

Tiramisù
Tiramisu

Servings: 8 people

Ingredients (For a 12x8 inch baking pan)

- 26.46 oz mascarpone
- 5 very fresh eggs
- 8.82 oz savoiardi
- 4.23 oz sugar
- 10–11 oz coffee (mocha)

To decorate

- Bitter cocoa powder to taste
- Dark chocolate drops to taste

DIRECTIONS:

1. Brew the coffee with a mocha to make 10–11 oz and let it cool in a shallow, wide bowl.
2. Separate the eggs by separating the whites from the yolks (put the yolks in one bowl and the whites in another), remember that to whip the egg whites well they should not have any trace of yolk.
3. Whip the egg yolks with electric whips, pouring in only half the sugar.
4. As soon as the mixture becomes light and frothy, and with the whisk still running, add the mascarpone, a little at a time. Once you have incorporated all the cheese you will have obtained a dense and compact cream; keep it aside.
5. Wash the whisk well and whip the egg whites. When they are frothy pour in the remaining sugar a little at a time. You will have to whip them until they are stiff; you will obtain this result when you turn the bowl upside down and the egg whites will remain on the bottom.
6. Take 1 tbsp of egg whites and pour it into the bowl with the mascarpone cream and mix vigorously with a spatula, so you're going to dilute the mixture.
7. Add the remaining egg whites, a little at a time mixing very gently from the bottom up. The mascarpone cream is now ready.
8. Spread a generous spoonful in the bottom of a glass baking dish, 12 x 8 inches, spread it out well with a spoon.
9. Dip the ladyfingers in the cold coffee for a few moments, first on one side and then on the other. Gradually distribute the soaked ladyfingers in an orderly manner in the oven dish, trying to arrange them all in one direction, so as to obtain a first layer of biscuits.
10. Add more mascarpone cream and level it to cover the ladyfingers completely.
11. Continue to distribute the ladyfingers soaked in coffee, then make another layer of cream and level the surface well.
12. Once you have created the last layer of ladyfingers, pour the remaining cream. Sprinkle with a handful of chocolate chips and some unsweetened cocoa powder and leave to harden in the fridge for at least 4 hours.
13. After 4 hours the tiramisu is ready to be enjoyed!

TIPS:

You can keep the tiramisu for a maximum of 2 days in the fridge, this is because the eggs are used raw and after 2 days they lose their freshness, they could alter the taste of the tiramisu and create digestive problems.
You can also create single portions of tiramisu, by assembling the dessert directly into individual cups or bowls.

Cantucci
Cantucci

Servings: 30 pieces

Ingredients

- 6.35 oz sugar
- 1 egg
- 0.015 oz ammonia for cakes
- 9.35 oz flour
- Almonds
- 0,35 oz marsala or other fortified wine
- ½ orange peel
- 1 pinch fine salt
- 1.06 oz room temperature butter (soft)

For brushing

- 1 egg yolk

DIRECTIONS:

1. To prepare the cantucci, start by putting the sugar in a bowl and add the egg with a pinch of salt. Mix with a spatula: there's no need to beat, just to melt the crystals well.
2. Separately, in another bowl, combine the flour and cake ammonia. Mix and add the dry ingredients to the egg and sugar mixture. Mix and add the soft butter as well.
3. Knead with your hands and add the almonds, then season with Marsala wine and the grated rind of half an orange. Knead until all the ingredients are well incorporated into the dough, then form a ball and transfer it onto the work surface.
4. Divide the loaf into 2 equal parts and make a long, rather narrow loaf from each.
5. Arrange the loaves well-spaced out on a baking tray covered with greaseproof paper (there is no need to flatten them, this will happen naturally during baking).
6. Brush the loaves with beaten egg yolk (if the yolk is too thick, you can dilute it with a little water).
7. Bake the loaves in a static oven preheated to 400°F for 20 minutes, then take them out of the oven and let them cool a few minutes.
8. Now, with a knife with a serrated blade, cut the filoncino slightly diagonally, creating cantucci about 0.4 inches thick. Arrange them again on the baking sheet covered with parchment paper and toast them in a static oven preheated to 320°F for 18 minutes.
9. Bake the cantucci and let them cool before enjoying.

TIPS:

Although she never finished her studies, my grandmother Lucia was a very cultured woman and loved to read. One day she told me that Herman Hesse, after having tasted the cantucci said that they were so good that they brought back his good mood! This typical Tuscan sweet is perfect for any occasion, especially if accompanied and dipped in a good glass of Vin Santo.

Cannoli Sicialiani
Sicilian Cannoli

Servings: 30 pieces

Ingredients

- 9.17 oz flour
- 0.7 oz sugar
- 1.06 oz lard cold from the refrigerator
- 0.7 oz bitter cocoa powder
- 1 tsp fine salt
- 0.70 oz egg
- 0.35 oz white wine vinegar
- 2.17 oz marsala

For the stuffing

- 35.27 oz sheep's milk ricotta (drained for at least 1 night in the fridge)
- 4.59 oz sugar
- 2,82 oz dark chocolate chips

For brushing

- Eggs to taste

For frying

- 4 cups seed oil

To garnish

- Candied cherries to taste
- Icing sugar to taste
- Pistachios grains to taste
- Candied orange to taste

DIRECTIONS:

1. To prepare the Sicilian cannoli start with the wafer: in a bowl pour the flour, sifted cocoa, sugar, salt and cold lard.
2. Take the egg and beat it lightly, then use 0.7 oz of it to put in the bowl with the other ingredients (keep the rest aside that will be used to brush on the cannoli later).
3. Then pour in the marsala and vinegar. Start mixing with your hands, then transfer to a work surface and knead for about ten minutes until you get a smooth dough. It will take a little patience and energy because the mixture will be rather dry.
4. Cover the dough with plastic wrap and let it rest in the fridge for about 1 hour, then take it out of the fridge and let it sit at room temperature for 30 minutes.
5. After the time has elapsed, take the dough, divide it in half. Take one of the two halves, leaving the other well covered, and lightly flour both sides. Press well with your hands and then insert the piece between the rollers of the pasta machine. It may tear at first, don't worry, just put the dough back together and repeat. As soon as it is well compact, fold the two ends inwards and pass again between the rollers starting with the larger thickness. Repeat 3–4 times, turning the dough in the opposite direction if necessary.
6. As soon as it is smoother, close the sheet this time not making two folds but only one and pass it through the rollers 3–4 more times.
7. At this point fold the sheet again, this time on the short side and pass it again between the rollers. Gradually decrease the thickness of the pasta machine. If you notice that the sheet is stretching too much divide it before proceeding. Keep stretching until you reach number 8 on the machine or what on your machine corresponds to a thickness of 0.02 inches. All of these steps will serve to make the dough more stretched out so that bubbles will form when baking.
8. Once you have the thickness of the sheet indicated, you can divide it in half for convenience. Trim the edges and add them to the other half of the dough that you still have aside.
9. With a smooth-bladed pastry cutter, cut out 4 x 4-inch squares, then take each square of dough in your hand, slide your thumbs from the center outward to slightly and gently spread it out; in the middle arrange a steel cylinder so that it goes from corner to corner.
10. Wrap one flap of dough over the cylinder, brush the other flap with the remaining egg before joining it with the other. You have formed the first cannoli, continue in this way with all the remaining dough.
11. It's important to let the cannoli sit for a while to air dry before baking.
12. Heat the oil until it reaches a temperature of 350°F. Fry the cannoli one at a time, placing them on a skimmer and holding them submerged for a few moments. This way they won't touch the bottom of the pan and burn. It will take less than 1 minute, turn them continuously.

13. Drain the cannoli, using tongs, and transfer them to a tray lined with kitchen paper. Then let them cool before removing the cylinder; to do this, simply press it lightly, the two metal sheets will tend to fit together. Then make a slight movement in the opposite direction to the closing direction of the cone and gently pull out the cylinder. At this point the cannoli shells are ready, keep them aside until they cool completely and in the meantime prepare the filling.
14. Sift the ricotta with a strainer into a bowl. Pour in the sugar and work the mixture with a spatula.
15. Add the chocolate chips and mix again. Transfer the cream into a piping bag and use it to fill the cannoli.
16. If you like, garnish the ends of the cannoli with chopped pistachios, candied orange peel or cherries and dust the cannoli with powdered sugar before serving!

TIPS:

The essence of Sicily contained in a single dessert. It seems a difficult preparation but it is not. You just need to pay attention to two things, as grandma Lucia used to say: stuff the cannoli just before serving them, in this way you will avoid softening the wafer that instead will remain nice and crispy; let the wafers cool well before stuffing them, otherwise the ricotta cream could decompose.

Zeppole di San Giuseppe Fritte
Zeppole di San Giuseppe Fried

Servings: 6 pieces

Ingredients

- 3 medium eggs
- 1 egg yolk
- 1.94 oz butter
- ½ cup water
- 5.3 oz flour
- Salt up to taste

For frying and garnishing

- 6 Amarena cherries in syrup
- Peanut seed oil to taste
- Icing sugar to taste

For 12.35 oz of custard

- 2 yolks
- 0.79 oz cornstarch (cornflour)
- ½ vanilla pod
- 2.47 oz sugar
- 0.83 cup whole milk
- 0.20 cup fresh liquid cream

DIRECTIONS:

1. Start by preparing the custard to fill the zeppole, so that it cools. Heat the milk and cream in a saucepan along with the vanilla bean and the seeds that you have previously extracted with a small knife.
2. When it comes to a boil, turn it off and keep warm.
3. In a small bowl lightly beat the egg yolks and pour in the sugar, then stir to combine the ingredients, then add the cornstarch and mix well.
4. Remove the vanilla pod from the milk and cream mixture, pour some of the milk and cream into the small bowl with the eggs, sugar and starch so that the mixture is diluted, mix well and then add the whole mixture into the saucepan with the milk and cream.
5. Turn the heat on low and stir continuously with a whisk until the cream has thickened. This will take about 10 minutes. Once ready you can place the cream in a shallow bowl and cover it with clingfilm. Leave to cool at room temperature and then in the fridge. Once chilled, you can transfer it to a disposable piping bag with a star-shaped nozzle.
6. Move on to the choux pastry: pour the water into a large saucepan, then add the chopped butter and a pinch of salt.
7. Turn the heat to medium and stir with a wooden spoon to melt the butter.
8. When the liquid begins to boil, pour in the amount of flour at once and keep stirring. The mixture should pull away from the sides of the pan.
9. At that point turn off the heat and pour it into a bowl. Spread out the center slightly to cool it faster and, separately, beat together the 3 whole eggs with the yolk.
10. Pour the egg mixture into the bowl with the mixture a little at a time, stirring constantly with a wooden spoon. At first, it will seem difficult to mix the eggs with the rest, it will take a little patience to get a smooth and homogeneous consistency; the mixture will eventually be quite fluid and creamy.
11. Pour it into a piping bag with a 0.45-inch star nozzle.
12. In a large saucepan heat the peanut oil and bring it to a temperature not exceeding 325°F; while the oil heats up, place on the work surface a tray covered with a sheet of baking paper on which you are going to create the zeppole well-spaced out (with these doses you will get 6).
13. With the sac-a´ poche draw a circle of dough in double turn, one circle on top of the other. The doughnut you are going to create should be about 2.3–2.7 inches in diameter.

14. Then cut out some squares of baking paper around the zeppole, so that they are easier to pick up and dive into the oil at the right temperature: one or maximum 2 zeppoles at a time with the side of the baking paper facing upwards. You will see that after a few moments the parchment paper will come off very easily (use a fork or tweezers to remove it); let the zeppole fry for a few minutes without turning them upside down so that they keep their shape while cooking.
15. Then flip the zeppole over and cook them on the other side as well. 5–6 minutes in all will be enough. Once they are ready and well browned, drain them with a skimmer. Place them on a tray lined with absorbent paper so that they release the excess oil. Continue in the same way as the others.
16. Take the sour cherries in syrup and set them aside.
17. When the zeppole have cooled (let them rest for at least 10–15 minutes), sprinkle them with icing sugar, then add a generous dollop of custard inside, lay the black cherries on top and sprinkle with icing sugar again.
18. Your fried zeppole di San Giuseppe is ready to be enjoyed!

TIPS:

On March 19 in Italy, we celebrate St. Joseph and also Father's Day and this cake is the symbol.
I still make zeppole for Father's Day, just like grandma taught me. They are so good and simple to prepare that sometimes I make them even without any holiday to celebrate.

Graffe
Neapolitan Staples

Servings: 12 staples

Ingredients

- 17.63 oz flour
- 9.88 oz potatoes
- 1.76 oz sugar
- 1.76 oz butter
- 0.42 cup milk
- 1 lemon peel
- 2 eggs
- 0.21 oz fresh brewer's yeast
- Peanut seed oil to taste

DIRECTIONS:

1. Melt the butter (in a double boiler or microwave) and let it cool completely.
2. Put the potatoes with the skins on in a pot of cold water and cook until cooked through and soft.
3. Drain the potatoes and mash them in a bowl while they are still hot with a potato masher (this way you won't have to remove the skin; if you don't have a potato masher, first peel the potatoes and then mash them with a fork) then add the butter and let it mix with the still hot potatoes.
4. Warm the milk in a saucepan, as soon as it is lukewarm pour it into a bowl and dissolve the crumbled brewer's yeast in it.
5. Add to the milk and yeast also the sugar, the grated rind of a lemon and mix well.
6. Add the whole eggs previously mixed with a fork.
7. Add potatoes.
8. Mix everything again and finally add the flour little by little mixing first with a fork and then kneading with your hands in order to obtain a homogeneous and elastic dough.
9. Transfer dough to floured work surface and knead well for 10 minutes until smooth.
10. Put the dough for the Neapolitan graffe in a bowl and cover it with a clean cloth and let it rise for 2 hours in a warm place (the oven off and closed is more than fine).
11. After the leavening time has elapsed, take the dough and deflate it with your hands, then thin it out (do not use a rolling pin, you could remove too much air from the dough) until it is about one finger thick.
12. Create some rounds with a glass, which will be the outer shape of the staple and to create the hole in the center use the cap of a bottle (if you have them you can easily use different sized pasta cups).
13. Place all the doughnuts you have created on a baking tray covered with greaseproof paper and leave them to rise for another 45 minutes covered with a tea towel.
14. When the graffe has risen completely, heat plenty of peanut oil and, when it is hot, fry one or 2 graffe at a time so that the oil temperature does not drop too much.
15. Prepare a large tray or plate, covered with plenty of caster sugar.
16. Drain the Neapolitan graffe on paper towels and dip them immediately in the caster sugar so that it sticks and lay the graffe on a clean tray.
17. Your graffe is ready to be served!

TIPS:

Neapolitan graffe is a typical Carnival sweet. I still remember the smell you could smell in the alleys of Naples on Carnival morning.

I prepare fried graffe for birthdays and also for Halloween and often, on this occasion, I also fill them with berry jam to give a blood-red effect that comes out from the graffe: I prepare the jam or I buy it ready-made, I pour it in a piping bag with a long syringe and, once the graffe are fried and cooled, I pierce them with the piping bag's mouth filling them with a little bit of jam. They are even tastier!

Babà
Neapolitan Baba

Servings: Quantity for 1 mold of 9 inches (typical mold for a baba or a doughnut mold with a hole in the center)

For the dough

- 14.1 oz flour
- 8 eggs
- 2.47 oz butter
- 2 tsp dry brewer's yeast or 0.42 oz fresh brewer's yeast
- 1.06 oz sugar
- 0.35 oz salt
- 1 sachet of vanilla

For the bath

- 2 cups water
- 0.5 cup dark rum
- 8.81 oz sugar
- Thick peel of 1 lemon

To serve

- Whipped cream to taste
- Strawberries or fruit of your choice to taste

TO PREPARE THE BABÀ TO PERFECTION YOU NEED A PLANETARY MIXER OR A KNEADING MACHINE.

DIRECTIONS:

1. First of all, put the flour, sugar and vanilla in the bowl of the planetary mixer, add the dry brewer's yeast, and if you are using the fresh one dilute it first with a tsp of water. Then mix with the whisk in the shape of K and add in 3 times the eggs. Always allow the previous eggs to be absorbed before adding more. The dough will be sticky, this is normal, keep working on medium-high speed until it clings to the whisk.
2. Add the chopped soft butter and mix well, finally add the salt. It will take about 10 minutes, slowly you will see the dough become more and more elastic.
3. Transfer the mixture to a bowl, don't worry if it sticks to your hands. Cover with plastic wrap and let rise for about 4 hours in an oven with the light off, until it quadruples in volume.
4. Once the dough has risen, transfer it to the previously buttered mould. Don't worry if it sticks, this is normal.
5. Finally leave to rise in the oven with the light on until the dough reaches the edge of the mould.
6. Then bake in a very hot static oven in the middle at 400°F for the first 10 minutes, then lower the temperature to 350°F and bake for about 5–8 more minutes! Do the toothpick test to check for doneness: the toothpick should come out dry.
7. While the baba is cooking, prepare the syrup by bringing the water and sugar to a boil in a saucepan.
8. When the sugar has completely dissolved after stirring continuously, turn off the heat and add the rum. Stir and let completely cool to room temperature.
9. Finally, when the Baba is ready, take it out of the oven and leave it to cool for at least 2 hours. For perfect dunking, the baba must be cold.
10. Put the Baba directly into a large, high-sided container.
11. First, slowly drizzle the top surface and sides with the sauce, until the entire amount of sauce has been poured over the entire baba.
12. The baba will then be completely submerged in the liquid. Gently press the baba and repeat the operation several times, pouring off the liquid and sponging the baba well so that it is actually soaked!
13. Once soaked, place the baba on a tray with edges at least 2 cm high and pour a few spoonfuls of the syrup on the bottom.
14. Decorate the Baba with clumps of whipped cream and fresh seasonal fruit, peeled and cut as you like.
15. The Neapolitan baba is ready!

TIPS:

Grandma Lucia always used to say that we have the French to thank for the Babà because it is an amazing goodness that originated in France; it was imported around 1800 to Naples and over time has become a Neapolitan symbol like the Pastiera, Zeppole or Sfogliatelle.
It may seem difficult to prepare, but it is not. However, it is essential to use the Planetary Mixer or the Kneading Machine, otherwise, the dough will never be "boiling" and swollen like the traditional one.

Torta Caprese
Caprese Cake

Servings: 10 peoples

For an 8-inch mold

- 6 oz 50% dark chocolate to grate
- 3 oz peeled almonds (to be reduced to powder)
- 3 oz whole peeled hazelnuts (to be reduced to powder)
- 6 oz icing sugar
- 6 oz softened butter
- 0.88 oz potato starch
- 0.5 oz bitter cocoa powder
- 5.22 oz egg whites at room temperature
- 3 oz egg yolks at room temperature
- 0.14 oz baking powder
- ½ bourbon vanilla pod
- Salt up to taste

To decorate

- Icing sugar to taste

DIRECTIONS:

1. To prepare the Caprese Cake, start by pouring the room temperature butter (it is best to leave it out of the fridge for at least 12 hours), half the sugar and the seeds scraped from half a vanilla pod with a small knife into a bowl.
2. Whisk at medium-high speed and after 6–7 minutes add the pinch of salt and egg yolks. The eggs should also be left at room temperature for at least 12 hours.
3. After a few minutes, the mixture will be frothy so turn off the whisk, clean the bowl with a spatula collecting all the mixture and keep aside.
4. In another bowl mix the powders: combine the grated chocolate, almonds powder and hazelnuts powder (you can reduce the nuts to powder directly with a blender). Then sift in the potato starch, baking powder and bitter cocoa powder.
5. Mix everything well and set aside.
6. In another bowl, pour the egg whites and remaining powdered sugar. Make sure that the whips are well cleaned, otherwise, the egg whites will not whip and will act. After a few minutes, the mixture will be shiny and frothy: you don't have to whip it stiff but the mixture should be like cream.
7. All the preparations are completed, so preheat the oven to 325°F in fan mode and start mixing: add to the egg yolk and butter mixture a third of the beaten egg whites, then a third of the powders and mix well with the spatula, stirring gently from the bottom up. Gradually add another part of the egg whites and a third of the powder and continue in this way until you get a uniform mixture.
8. Pour the smooth, creamy mixture into an 8-inch cake pan already buttered and floured with potato starch. Carefully level the surface and bake in a 325°F ventilated oven for about 45 minutes.
9. Once baked, let the cake cool in the mold, then invert and unmold.
10. Turn it out again onto a plate lined with baking paper and let it cool completely.
11. Once cold, turn the cake upside down one last time, remove the baking paper and dust the surface of the cake with powdered sugar.
12. The Caprese Cake is ready to be enjoyed!

TIPS:

This is the traditional Neapolitan recipe for Caprese and my grandmother received it directly from a good friend of hers who is a pastry chef. An alternative version of the Caprese cake uses melted chocolate but in this case the result will be more compact. If you prefer you can try both versions and then choose the one you like best!

I also suggest you prepare the hazelnut and toasted almond flours in advance: just blend them at full speed with a blender, just long enough to refine them. Then pour the crumbs onto a sheet of baking paper and let them air dry overnight.

Pasta di Mandorle
Almond Pastes

Servings: 20 pieces

Ingredients

- 8.80 oz whole peeled almonds
- 8.80 oz sugar
- 2 egg whites
- ½ tsp almond flavoring

To garnish

- Candied cherries to taste
- Whole almonds to taste

DIRECTIONS:

1. To prepare the almond paste, place the peeled almonds and the sugar in a blender fitted with steel blades and blend until they turn into a powder. Remember that this step should only take a few minutes to prevent the almonds from overheating and releasing their oil.
2. Add the egg whites and the almond flavoring and whisk again to mix everything together. The mixture will be ready when it is firm but soft to the touch, then transfer it into a strong piping bag with a 0.4-inch ribbed nozzle.
3. Line a baking sheet with baking paper.
4. With the sac-à-poche form little piles with a diameter of 1,2 inches and high of about 0.8 inches and garnish part of them with candied cherries cut in half and another part with whole almonds.
5. At this point, place the pan in the refrigerator and let the almond pastries cool for at least 7 hours (or even better overnight), covering them with plastic wrap.
6. After this time has elapsed, take the pan back out, and bake in a preheated ventilated oven at 350°F for about 15 minutes, placing the pan on the medium rack. Be careful not to overcook them, otherwise, they won't be soft enough inside: they should still turn out a little pale.
7. Once baked, let them cool before serving.

TIPS:

Almond Pastes are perfect to enjoy after coffee or to accompany the moment of tea, their characteristic is the extreme sweetness and texture that remains crispier on the outside and softer on the inside.

Biscotti all'Amarena
Amarena Cookies

Servings: 9 people

For the sponge cake

- 3 eggs
- 1.8 oz flour
- 0.9 oz cornstarch
- 2.4 oz sugar

For the pastry

- 14 oz flour
- 5.3 oz butter
- 5.3 oz sugar
- 3 yolks
- 1 egg white
- 1 pinch of fine salt

For the stuffing

- 10,5 black cherry jam
- 7 oz sponge cake
- 1 oz bitter cocoa powder
- 1 egg yolk

For the icing

- 5.3 icing sugar
- 1 egg white
- 1 tsp lemon juice

To decorate

- 0.5 oz black cherry jam

DIRECTIONS:

1. Start with the sponge cake. Pour the eggs into the bowl of a planetary mixer. Start working them with the whisk and add the sugar. Whip the mixture until foamy and fluffy. It will take about 15 minutes.
2. Meanwhile, butter and flour an 8-inch mould.
3. When the eggs are well whipped, remove the bowl from the mixer and sift the cornstarch and flour directly into it. Mix with a spatula from the bottom up with very delicate movements to avoid disassembling the mixture. When you have obtained a uniform mixture pour it inside the mould and bake in a static oven preheated to 350°F for 25 minutes on the central shelf.
4. Always do the toothpick test before taking the cake out of the oven. Once cooked, take the sponge cake out of the oven and, being careful not to burn yourself, turn it out immediately and let it cool completely on a wire rack.
5. While the sponge cake is cooling, make the shortcrust pastry. In the bowl of a planetary mixer fitted with the paddle attachment, pour the butter cut into cubes and the sugar. Work the mixture until creamy, then add the egg white and wait until it is completely absorbed before adding the egg yolks. Knead for a couple more minutes until they are completely absorbed.
6. Still with the mixer running at moderate speed, add the flour and salt. Work again until the mixture is smooth.
7. At this point, transfer the dough onto a flat surface, shape it into a loaf and wrap it in plastic wrap. Leave to rest in the fridge for at least 1 hour.
8. When the sponge cake is completely cold and the shortcrust pastry has almost finished firming up in the fridge you can start preparing the filling.
9. Crumble the sponge cake inside a bowl, you will need 7 oz.
10. Then add the egg yolk, cocoa and black cherry jam. Knead everything with your hands until you get a smooth and soft mixture.
11. Transfer to a sheet of baking paper that you have placed on the work surface. Give the mixture a rectangular shape and place it in the fridge for 30 minutes.
12. When the shortcrust pastry has rested, take the dough and roll it out on a lightly floured surface until you obtain a square about 0.2 inches thick.
13. Then place the sour cherry mixture in the center of the rectangle, remove the baking paper and, using a smooth-bladed knife, even out the edges of the pastry so that the 2 edges cover the filling without overlapping.
14. You can freeze the excess shortcrust pastry wrapped in plastic wrap to make cookies.
15. When you have eliminated the excess, fold the 2 flaps towards the center and lightly pinch the dough with your fingers to make them adhere perfectly.
16. Turn out onto a tray lined with baking paper and place in the refrigerator for at least 10 minutes.

17. During these 10 minutes, also prepare the frosting. Pour the egg whites into a bowl and add the lemon juice. Then start working with an electric whisk adding the icing sugar a little at a time until you get a thick icing.
18. Then take the loaf and with a knife remove the part of dough without filling. Place a little icing in the center and spread it over the whole surface.
19. Once you have completely covered the loaf, using a toothpick create a cavity all along one side about 0,4 inches from the edge. Do the same thing for the other side.
20. Then make a cone out of baking paper and fill it with the jam. Then use it to fill the grooves just created with the toothpick.
21. At this point, all that's left to do is cut out cookies about 1.4 inches wide. Arrange them as you go on a baking tray lined with baking paper and bake in a static oven preheated to 330°F on the middle shelf for 20–25 minutes.
22. Bake the black cherry cookies and let them cool before serving.

TIPS:

To prepare these cookies will take a little patience, the preparations are many, but all very simple. Do not be discouraged, the taste will repay all your efforts!
My grandmother used to tell me that in her day, a black cherry biscuit cost a few lire because the bakeries made them using all the scraps from other preparations.
I make these cookies in industrial quantities at Christmas: I buy tins and give them as gifts to friends and work colleagues, as black cherry cookies can be stored in a cool, dry place for up to 5–6 days.

Struffoli
Struffoli

Servings: 8 people

Ingredients

- 19.4 oz flour
- 0.7 oz sugar
- 1 pinch of fine salt
- 3.5 oz butter
- 3 eggs
- 2 yolks
- 0.14 oz baking soda
- 1 orange peel
- 0.88 oz aniseed liqueur
- 1 lemon peel

For frying

- Sunflower seed oil to taste

To season the struffoli

- 21 oz wildflower honey
- 3.5 oz sugar
- 1 lemon peel
- 1 orange peel
- Colored tails to taste
- 5.3 oz diced candied orange
- Candied cherries to taste
- Decoration food silver sprinkles to taste

DIRECTIONS:

1. To prepare the struffoli start by sifting the flour on the pastry board and widening it to form the classic fountain. Add the salt.
2. Combine the sugar and baking soda. Cut the butter into cubes and arrange it in the center.
3. Start mixing the butter with the sugar with your hands, then add the eggs in the center one at a time and continue to knead adding the yolks.
4. Now pour in the aniseed liqueur, the lemon and orange peel, both grated
5. Start working the dough with your hands to obtain a smooth and homogeneous dough. Wrap the dough with plastic wrap so it doesn't dry out. Let rest for 30 minutes at room temperature.
6. Remove one part of the dough, keeping the other part well covered. Shape loaves 0.4 inches thick and cut out small pieces about 0,4–0,6 inches wide.
7. Gradually transfer them onto a tray lined with a clean tea towel, spacing them out. Continue in this way until the dough is finished, spacing the pieces well apart.
8. Move on to frying: pour the oil into a large pot and heat it up to a temperature of 300–320°F. Dip the struffoli a few pieces at a time, using a slotted spoon and shake them a little during cooking, so they will be round.
9. When they are well browned, drain them; it will take about 3–4 minutes. Transfer them on a tray with kitchen paper to remove excess oil and continue in this way for the cooking of all the other struffoli.
10. Garnish: Take the candied orange and cut it into cubes.
11. Separately, pour the honey and sugar into a saucepan. Heat over low heat stirring occasionally. As soon as it starts to boil, turn off the heat. Let it cool and add the lemon and orange zest, both grated. Add the diced candied orange and mix again.
12. Let cool for 5–6 minutes, then pour the struffoli inside. Mix well with a wooden spoon until the struffoli is well coated and cooled.
13. Transfer to a serving dish, decorate with the colored sprinkles, candied orange peel and candied cherries. The struffoli are ready!

TIPS:

In my house it's not Christmas without Struffoli!
These are the most characteristic Neapolitan sweets of the Christmas period.
As for the origins of struffoli, we have to go back to the age of the ancient Greeks who seem to have exported them to the

Gulf of Naples at the time of Partenope. And it is from the greek that according to many would also derive the name "struffoli": more precisely from the word "strongoulos", or "rounded".
I still remember when I used to prepare them with my grandmother; she used to make me round them because she said that, with my small hands, I could give them the perfect shape.

Sbrisolona
Sbrisolona

Servings: 8 peoples

For an 11-inch mold

- 7.8 oz flour
- 3.5 oz cornmeal
- 7 oz almond flour
- 7 oz soft butter
- 7 oz sugar
- 2 eggs
- 1.4 oz almonds
- 1 oz maraschino
- 0.35 oz baking powder
- ½ vanilla pod
- A pinch of fine salt

TO MAKE THE SBRISOLONA CAKE YOU'LL NEED UNPEELED ALMOND FLOUR, WHICH YOU CAN FIND AT ANY CAKE SUPPLY STORE.

DIRECTIONS:

1. Place the flour and baking powder, cornmeal and almond flour on the work surface. Create the classic fountain. In the center put the soft but still plastic butter, salt, eggs, and sugar and start working the ingredients in the center with your hands.
2. Add maraschino liqueur and raw almonds chopped very coarsely. Continue working with your hands, add the seeds of the vanilla pod.
3. At this point work the powders "crosswise", that is, bringing the ingredients from the outside to the inside, handling them and mixing them with the rest. You will obtain a homogeneous consistency in a few moments.
4. At this point, transfer the dough onto a baking tray lined with greaseproof paper and flatten it with your hands. Transfer to the freezer to chill the dough for at least 4 hours.
5. As soon as the dough is firm and you have a stiff block, make the dough crumbs. Place a grid with 0.4-inch square holes on a bowl, cut the dough into pieces and crush it by passing it through the grid. This way you will get big crumbs.
6. Take a flared aluminum mold that measures 12–13 inches on top and 11 inches on the bottom; place a circle of parchment paper inside and pour the crumbs inside.
7. Spread it out gently without pressing it down. Bake in a preheated 325°F static oven for 45 minutes until golden brown.
8. Remove from the oven and leave to cool before unmolding and serving the sbrisolona cake.

TIPS:

The sbrisolona cake is a typical Lombardy sweet, the pride of the city of Mantua: it is a hard cake, with a rich flavor that is made and served in coarse pieces. Hence the name sbrisolona, from "sbrisa" or crumb. This recipe is a demonstration of how simple it is to prepare this cake of peasant origins, which is now very popular abroad, so much so that it is an Italian culinary heritage.

Baci di Dama
Lady Kisses

Servings: 125 pieces

Ingredients

- 10.5 oz butter
- 10.5 oz sugar
- 10.5 oz almond flour
- 10.5 oz flour
- 1 egg white
- 0.1 oz fine salt

To make

- 13 oz Dark tempered chocolate
  (alternatively hazelnut spread)

DIRECTIONS:

1. Start with the shortcrust pastry. In the bowl of a planetary mixer fitted with the paddle attachment, pour the soft but still plastic cubed butter and the sugar. Let it run a few seconds on low speed until the dough is well mixed.
2. Add the almond flour and run the planetary mixer again.
3. Pour egg whites into a bowl, add salt to dissolve. Pour everything into the dough.
4. As soon as the fat mass is well blended, turn off the machine and add the sifted flour. Always mix at low speed, eventually cleaning the edges of the planetary mixer with a spatula after a few seconds.
5. As soon as the flour has been absorbed, transfer the dough to a lightly floured surface. Add a light layer of flour and compact it without kneading. Wrap the dough with plastic wrap and transfer to the refrigerator for 2–3 hours.
6. When the dough is well stabilized move it to a lightly floured surface. Using two rulers, roll out the dough with a rolling pin to an even thickness of 0,4 inches. Trim the first edge, then cut strips lengthwise 0.8 inches thick using a ruler and knife.
7. Make the lattice by making strips 0.8 inches wide in the other direction, so that you make cubes that will weigh about 0.14–0.16 inches each.
8. Round them off in the palm of a hand and place on a baking tray lined with greaseproof paper, spacing them out.
9. Bake in a preheated static oven at 350°F for 12 minutes. As soon as the cookies are golden brown, take them out of the oven and let them cool.
10. Now temper the chocolate and transfer it inside a baking paper cone.
11. Turn half of the half spheres upside down, squeeze a little chocolate in the center. Place another half sphere on top, pressing lightly so that they are joined. Repeat this operation for all the cookies and let them solidify at room temperature before enjoying them. If it gets too hot store the baci di dama in the fridge.

TIPS:

How to temper dark chocolate?
Chop the dark chocolate, then melt it in a double boiler. When the chocolate has reached a temperature of 129°F pour 2/3 of it on a marble slab placed on a work surface and work the chocolate on the marble slab, with a spatula and a scraper, spreading it on the surface. When it has reached 82°F, transfer it to the bowl where you left the remaining chocolate and mix: the chocolate should reach 87–89°F. If during these phases the temperature should drop too much, always keep the pot with hot water on hand to slightly heat the chocolate (always in a bain-marie). On the contrary, if it is still too hot, spatula some of the chocolate back onto the marble.

Crostata di Albicocche
Tart With Apricot Jam

Servings: 8 peoples

For an 8-inch mold

- 8.8 oz flour
- 5.3 oz butter (soft, but still plastic)
- 3.5 oz icing sugar
- 5 egg yolks
- 0.7 oz acacia honey
- ½ lemon peel
- ½ vanilla pod
- 0,03 oz fine salt

For the stuffing

- 8.8 oz apricot jam
- ½ lemon peel

DIRECTIONS:

1. First of all, make the shortcrust pastry. In the bowl of a planetary mixer fitted with the paddle attachment, pour the soft but still plastic butter. Add the icing sugar, the seeds taken from the vanilla pod and the grated lemon zest. Run the machine at a low speed and add the honey.
2. In a separate small bowl pour the egg yolks and salt, stir to dissolve.
3. Add everything to the planetary mixer and when you get a uniform buttery mass, turn off the machine and incorporate the sifted flour in 2 times, always mixing at low speed. You will have to work the dough as little as possible: it should be soft, but not sticky.
4. At this point, lightly flour the worktop and transfer the shortcrust pastry, using a spatula. Add some more flour on top and without kneading, compact the dough to form a loaf. Wrap in plastic wrap and place in the refrigerator to firm up, possibly overnight. In this way, the dough will stabilize and it will be much easier to work it.
5. The next day you can move on to the composition of the tart. Pour the jam into a bowl, add the grated lemon zest and mix with a spatula or a spoon.
6. Take the shortcrust pastry from the fridge, remove the foil and place it on a lightly floured surface. Add some more flour on top of the pastry and roll it out with a rolling pin to a thickness of 0.13 inches. The thickness should be uniform, passing the dough between the 2 inches you will notice if there are thicker parts.
7. At this point cup the dough using an 8-inch ring.
8. Place the ring on a baking tray lined with baking paper, transfer the disc of dough inside and prick the base with the tines of a fork.
9. Pour the jam into the center of the pastry disk and spread it out with the back of a spoon, leaving about 0.4 inches from the clean edge.
10. Cut strips from the remaining shortcrust pastry.
11. Add a little more flour on top of the dough for the strips and give a stroke of the rolling pin, the thickness of the strips should be slightly less than the base of the tart. To cut out the strips, use a rolling pin and a smooth pastry wheel. Place the strips on the tart, first in one direction and then in the other. Remove the excess with light pressure. Make the lattice not too wide, this is important so that the jam does not burn and the tart cooks perfectly.
12. With the remaining shortcrust pastry, create a stick 0.8 inches in diameter and place it around the entire circumference of the tart. Crush it lightly with your fingertips. Using the handle of a spoon, imprint pressure all over the edge. In this way, you will join the 2 parts of dough and at the same time create a decoration.
13. Bake the tart in a static oven at 320°F for 45 minutes on the lowest rack (not the bottom). When golden brown, take it out of the oven and let it cool before removing the ring.
14. Once completely cooled, you can serve your apricot jam tart.

Amaretti
Macaroons

Servings: 50 pieces

Ingredients

- 7 oz peeled almonds
- 5 oz sugar
- 4.4 oz icing sugar
- 1.75 oz egg white
- 0.5 almonds
- 0.1 oz ammonia for sweets (or baking soda)
- Bitter almond extract to taste

DIRECTIONS:

1. To make the macaroons, toast the peeled almonds for 3 minutes in a static oven preheated to 400°F.
2. Then pour them into the mixer with the almonds, caster sugar and icing sugar and chop everything.
3. Then sift the mixture before pouring it back into the blender to chop it even finer. Sift it again into a large bowl.
4. Now add the cake ammonia, the egg whites and a few drops of almond extract. Mix with a spatula to amalgamate the ingredients and obtain a soft and homogeneous mixture.
5. Cover with a clean tea towel and place the dough in the refrigerator overnight.
6. The following day, take the dough that has solidified and cut out about 50 balls.
7. You can bake in two batches, arranging 25 balls at a time spaced apart on a baking sheet lined with parchment paper. Crush them lightly in the center with your fingers and bake in a static oven preheated to 325°F for about 20 minutes (300°F for 10–15 minutes in a fan oven).
8. Once the necessary time has passed, take the macaroons out of the oven and leave them to cool on a grill before offering them to your guests.

APPETIZERS AND BRUNCH

Salsa Tzatziki
Tzatziki Sauce

Servings: 4 peoples

Ingredients

- 14 oz white greek yogurt
- 6 oz cucumbers
- 2 cloves of garlic
- 1 tbsp extra virgin olive oil
- 1 tsp white wine vinegar
- Salt to taste

DIRECTIONS:

1. To make the tzatziki sauce, first, wash and remove the seeds from the cucumber.
2. Grate the cucumber with a wide-mesh grater, without removing the peel. Transfer the grated cucumber to a colander placed over a bowl and let it sit for at least 1 hour so that the vegetable water is removed.
3. After this time, peel the cloves of garlic and remove the soul with a knife, then chop them finely crushing them with the blade of the knife until you get a sort of cream. Alternatively, you can use a mortar with a pestle.
4. Pour the yogurt into a bowl, season with salt and add the oil, vinegar and mix well.
5. Now squeeze the cucumber by pressing with the back of a spoon to remove all the vegetation water and add it to the yogurt.
6. Finally, add the garlic cream and stir again.
7. Let the tzatziki sauce rest in the refrigerator for 2–3 hours covered with plastic wrap to allow the flavors to blend best. Stir gently before serving.

TIPS:

For a really perfect tzatziki sauce, as my mom makes, I recommend using a good quality Greek yogurt, as it will make the sauce tasty and full-bodied.
Serve the dip with appetizers like chicken nuggets, nachos or a pita.

Panzarotti Napoletani
Potato Croquettes

Servings: 30 pieces

Ingredients

- 35 oz red potatoes
- 1 oz egg yolks
- Nutmeg to taste
- Black pepper to taste
- Salt up to taste
- 3.5 oz grated parmesan cheese dop

For breading

- 2 eggs
- breadcrumbs to taste

For frying

- Peanut oil

DIRECTIONS:

1. To prepare the potato croquettes, wash the potatoes under running water to remove any earth residue, and put them to boil in a large saucepan, pouring water over them until they are completely covered, without peeling them: use potatoes of the same size as much as possible so that they are cooked evenly. It will take about 40 minutes.
2. Once ready, let them cool slightly (just long enough to handle) and then peel them.
3. Mash them in a potato masher to a puree while they are still hot.
4. In a separate small bowl beat the egg yolks with pepper and salt and then add them to the mashed potatoes, season with grated nutmeg and grated cheese, stir with a spoon to mix the ingredients until you get a soft and dry mixture.
5. Take a portion of dough weighing about 1.3 oz and form the croquettes into a cylindrical shape, with the two ends slightly flattened. As you form the croquettes, place them on a tray lined with baking paper.
6. Once you have finished the dough, knead the croquettes: Prepare two bowls, one with the 2 beaten eggs and the other with the breadcrumbs. Dip the croquettes first in the egg and then in the breadcrumbs. Lay the croquettes on a tray lined with baking paper.
7. Once all the croquettes are done, heat the peanut oil until it reaches 350°F and then dip 3–4 croquettes inside at a time so the oil temperature doesn't drop.
8. Cook, turning them with a skimmer until they are golden brown on all sides. Drain and place them on a plate lined with paper towels.
9. Serve the potato croquettes still warm!

TIPS:

For perfect croquettes, it is necessary to use the right potatoes and above all to work them when they are still hot, otherwise the croquettes will tend to break during frying.
If you want, you can add some chopped parsley to the potato mixture as well.

Arancini di Riso
Rice Arancini

Servings: 12 pieces (2 different fillings)

Ingredients

- 1 sachet saffron
- 1 oz butter
- 17.5 vialone nano rice
- 1 pinch fine salt
- 5 cups water
- 3.5 oz caciocavallo cheese to grate

For the prosciutto stuffing

- 1 oz cooked ham in one slice
- 2 oz mozzarella

For the batter

- 7 oz flour 00
- 1 pinch fine salt
- 1,25 cup water

For the meat sauce filling:
- Salt to taste
- Black pepper to taste
- ½ onion
- 0.9 oz butter
- 3.5 oz ground pork
- extra virgin olive oil to taste
- 0.8 cup tomato puree
- 2.8 oz peas
- 1.7 oz fresh caciocavallo cheese
- 0.2 cup red wine

For breading and frying

- Breadcrumbs to taste
- Seed oil to taste

DIRECTIONS:

1. Start by boiling the rice in salted boiling water, so that, when cooked, the water has been completely absorbed (this will allow the starch to remain all in the pot and you will get a very dry and compact rice).
2. Cook the rice for about 15 minutes, then dissolve the saffron in a little hot water and add it to the cooked rice. Add the butter in small pieces and the grated cheese, mix well to amalgamate everything, then pour and level the rice on a wide and low tray and cover with plastic wrap to let it cool completely. The foil will prevent the surface of the rice from drying out. Let the rice rest for a couple of hours outside the fridge.
3. In the meantime, dedicate yourself to the meat sauce filling: peel and finely slice the onion.
4. Stew the chopped onion in a pan with 2 tbsp of oil and the butter, then add the minced meat; brown it on a high flame, then add the wine and let it evaporate.
5. Add the tomato puree, add salt and pepper to taste and simmer covered for at least 20 minutes.
6. Halfway through cooking, add the peas.
7. While the peas are cooking, dice the caciocavallo cheese, cooked ham and mozzarella. This way all the fillings are ready!
8. Once the rice has cooled completely (this will take at least a couple of hours), you can form the arancini. To help you in the formation keep a bowl filled with water nearby so you can moisten your hands.
9. Take a couple of tbsp of rice at a time, crush the heap in the center of the palm of your hand forming a hollow and pour in a tsp of meat sauce filling and add a few cubes of caciocavallo cheese.
10. Then close the base of the arancino with the rice and shape it into a point: you can give this shape to all the arancini stuffed with meat sauce.
11. While for the ham filling, stuff each arancino with diced ham and mozzarella and shape them into a round shape.
12. Now that you have all the arancini ready, prepare the batter: in a bowl pour the sifted flour, a pinch of salt and the water. Mix thoroughly with a whisk to prevent lumps from forming.
13. Then dip the arancini entirely, one by one, first into the batter and then into a bowl with the breadcrumbs.
14. In a saucepan, heat the oil and bring it to a temperature of 350°F and fry one arancino at a time or a maximum of two so as not to lower the temperature of the oil: when they are well browned you can drain them and move them to a tray lined with paper towels.
15. Enjoy the rice arancini piping hot!

Frittatine di Pasta
Neapolitan Pasta Frittatine

Servings: 15 pieces

Ingredients

- 17.5 oz bucatini or spaghetti
- 5.3 oz cooked ham to be diced
- 2.6 oz frozen peas
- 1 clove of garlic
- Extra virgin olive oil to taste
- 6 cups peanut seed oil
- Salt up to taste

For the béchamel

- 7 oz flour
- 4.5 oz butter
- 4 cups whole milk
- Salt up to taste
- Nutmeg to taste

For the batter

- 1.4 cups water
- 7 oz flour

DIRECTIONS:

1. To prepare the Neapolitan frittatine pasta, start with the béchamel sauce. Heat the milk in a saucepan while melting the butter in another saucepan.
2. As soon as the butter is melted add the flour all at once and mix with a whisk until everything is compact. If it curdles quickly don't worry.
3. Then stir in the hot milk, pouring it in a little at a time, taking care that no lumps form.
4. Once the mixture is well blended, add salt and nutmeg and continue cooking until you get a nice firm cream. Transfer to a bowl, cover with cling film and leave to cool to room temperature.
5. Move on to the stuffing. Cut the ham into small cubes.
6. In the meantime, crush a clove of garlic and put it in a pan with a little oil. Sauté for a few moments over medium heat and then add the cubes of cooked ham and the peas. Sauté for a few moments, adjust the salt, remove the garlic and set everything aside.
7. At this point, you can cook the pasta in boiling salted water, take care to drain it when there are 2–3 minutes to the end of cooking. Pour it onto a lightly greased work surface, then add a drop of oil and mix quickly so as not to burn. Coarsely chop up the pasta with a knife and leave it to cool.
8. When all the ingredients are at room temperature, pour the béchamel sauce over the pasta. Knead well with your hands and then scoop out a handful.
9. Dig in the center and insert a handful of peas and ham. Close and squash well inside a 3-inch ramekin. Alternatively, you can also shape the fritters by hand.
10. Gradually lift the medallions with the help of a small spatula and then arrange them on a tray with baking paper. Remove the ring and start again, obtaining about 15 pieces.
11. When they are ready, let them cool in the fridge for at least an hour or until they are firm.
12. Heat the oil for frying and prepare the batter.
13. In a bowl put the flour, pour the water in a trickle while mixing with the whisk. Season with salt and continue to mix until you have a smooth batter without lumps.
14. Dip the first fritter. Drain the excess batter and dip the fritter into the hot oil, you can add more, but no more than 2–3 fritters at a time. This way the oil temperature will remain consistently at 360°F.
15. After 3–4 minutes they should be nicely browned, so drain them on paper towels and continue cooking all the others.
16. Here are your delicious Neapolitan pasta fritters ready!

Panino Napoletano
Neapolitan Sandwiches

Servings: 8 pieces

Ingredients

- 16 oz flour
- ½ cup water
- 4.4 oz whole milk
- 0.5 oz fresh brewer's yeast
- 0.7 oz extra virgin olive oil
- 0.3 oz fine salt

For brushing

- 0.7 oz fresh liquid cream
- 1 egg yolk

For the stuffing

- 5.3 oz mozzarella for pizza
- 3.5 oz mortadella whole piece
- 3.5 oz Neapolitan salami whole piece
- 4 eggs
- 1.4 oz parmesan cheese DOP to grate
- black pepper to taste

DIRECTIONS:

1. To prepare the Neapolitan rolls start with the dough. In a small pot mix water and milk, add the yeast and dissolve with a fork.
2. Pour the mixture into a bowl into which you poured the flour and mix with your hands.
3. Gradually add the oil and then the salt. As soon as the mixture has taken consistency transfer it to the worktop and work it for a few moments until smooth.
4. Move it to a bowl, cover it with plastic wrap and let it rise in a warm place at a constant temperature of about 80°F for a couple of hours or until doubled in volume.
5. In the meantime, boil the eggs for about 8 minutes; when they are hard-boiled, drain and peel them, then crumble them coarsely with a fork.
6. Cut the mortadella, Neapolitan salami and mozzarella into small cubes.
7. After the rising time, the dough will have doubled in volume. Transfer it to a lightly floured pastry board and roll it out with the aid of a rolling pin to obtain a sheet a little less than half an inch thick.
8. Spread the charcuterie over the top, leaving some free space around the edge.
9. Also add the eggs, mozzarella and grated Parmigiano, then grind plenty of black pepper.
10. Roll the pastry up into a large roll. Close the ends well and leave them to rest in the fridge for half an hour: this will make it easier to cut.
11. Once cooled, cut the roll into pieces about 1.7 inches thick.
12. Transfer the Panini onto a baking tray lined with baking paper and brush the surface with a little cream and egg yolk beaten together.
13. Bake the Neapolitan rolls in a static oven, preheated to 400°F, for about 35 minutes.
14. Let them cool for a few minutes before enjoying.

TIPS:

Panini Napoletani is great any way you choose to fill them. I also prepare an excellent vegetarian version, with sauteed vegetables such as peppers, zucchini, eggplant and a few cherry tomatoes; or with ricotta and spinach or even with 4 kinds of cheese.
Either way, they will be a very welcome course for your guests.

Pita Greca
Greek Pita

Servings: 4 pieces

For the pita dough

- 12.3 oz flour
- 0.8 cup water
- 1 tbsp olive oil
- 2 tsp fine salt
- 0.35 oz fresh brewer's yeast

For the condiment

- Salt to taste
- Oregano to taste
- Olive oil to taste

DIRECTIONS:

1. Prepare the dough by hand or with a planetary mixer: put the flour in a bowl.
2. Dissolve the brewer's yeast in room temperature water, neither cold nor warm.
3. Add the water and yeast to the flour and start kneading. Halfway through, add the olive oil and, only at the end, the salt. The dough should be soft and not sticky.
4. Shape into a loaf and place in a bowl covered with plastic wrap to rise until the dough doubles in volume. Depending on the temperature it may take about 1 hour or so.
5. Take the dough and divide it into 4 loaves. Roll them out to form flatbreads, by hand or with a rolling pin.
6. Dot the buns with your fingertips. Cover for 15 minutes with a clean cloth.
7. Heat a nonstick skillet and lightly grease it.
8. Lay the pita on top and cook, in the meantime brush the surface with olive oil, salt and oregano.
9. Turn it over halfway through cooking when the bottom is cooked through.
10. The oil should only be added to the first pita in the pan, not all of them.
11. Your pita is ready to be served warm, open or fanned closed with a filling.

TIPS:

The Greek Pita is an excellent substitute for bread and can be used to accompany main courses and salads of all kinds, chickpea hummus or rolled to stuff: my mom stuffs it with Greek salad made with feta cheese, cucumbers, tomatoes and tzatziki sauce, or she prepares delicious Gyros that are made with pork, tzatziki sauce and chips.
Of course, you can let your imagination run wild and enjoy it however you like.

Caponata
Caponata

Servings: 6 people

Ingredients	**To fry the eggplant**

Ingredients

- 35 oz eggplants
- 14 oz celery
- 8.8 oz white onions
- 7 oz ramato tomatoes
- 7 oz pitted green olives in brine
- 1.7 oz salted desalted capers
- 1.7 oz pine nuts
- 2 oz sugar
- 2 oz white wine vinegar
- Basil to taste
- 1.4 oz tomato concentrate
- Extra virgin olive oil to taste
- Salt to taste

To fry the eggplant

- Extra virgin olive oil to taste

DIRECTIONS:

1. To make the caponata, first peel the onion and slice it finely.
2. Stip the celery and cut it into rounds.
3. Halve the green olives and remove the stone inside.
4. Wash and dry the eggplants, trim them and then cut them into chunks. Do the same with the tomatoes.
5. Heat a frying pan and toast the pine nuts for a few minutes until golden brown.
6. Now take the eggplants: add the olive oil to a pan with a high rim and heat it, then pour a few eggplants at a time and fry them for a few minutes. Once they are golden brown, drain with a slotted spoon and place them on a tray lined with paper towels to remove excess oil, then set aside.
7. Pour a generous amount of olive oil into a large pan, heat it up and then add the onion. Fry well until the onion is wilted, then add the celery; let it brown well and then add the capers, olives, toasted pine nuts, and tomatoes. Sauté for a few moments, then cover with a lid and cook over low heat for 15–20 minutes.
8. Meanwhile, prepare the sweet and sour sauce: pour the vinegar, tomato paste, and sugar into a small pot. Mix well with a tsp and, after 15–20 minutes of cooking, add salt and pour the sauce into the pan.
9. Turn up the heat and stir until the hint of vinegar has evaporated.
10. Turn off the flame, add the fried eggplant and add the basil. Mix everything together, transfer the caponata to an ovenproof dish, let it cool and place it in the fridge, as the special feature of caponata is that it should be served cold or at room temperature: the next day it will be even better!

TIPS:

In Sicily, just move from province to province and everyone will have their own recipe for caponata: with or without raisins, with or without tomato paste, etc., but they all have an unmistakable common denominator: the use of the sweet and sour seasoning, which gives the vegetables a unique flavor.
This recipe is Grandma Lucia's and comes directly from her Sicilian relatives.

Freselle Napoletane
Freselle Napoletane

Servings: 6 pieces

Ingredients

- 14 oz flour
- ½ cube yeast (1 if it is winter)
- ½ tsp salt
- Tepid water

DIRECTIONS:

1. Put the flour in a bowl, gradually add the warm water in which the crumbled yeast has been dissolved. Mix all the ingredients, adding salt at the end and water as much as it absorbs.
2. Knead the dough for about 10 minutes until smooth and homogeneous.
3. Form into a ball and let the dough rest for 20 minutes.
4. Resume the dough and form it into loaves weighing about 7 oz.
5. With your hands make a hole in the center and spread them out to make wide, flattened doughnuts.
6. Let them rise for another 15–20 minutes on a sheet of baking paper and cover with a clean tea towel.
7. Put them in the oven and bake them for about 15–20 minutes at 320°F in a preheated oven, so that they dry out. After that time, take them out of the oven and let them cool.
8. When they are cold cut them horizontally with a knife and separate them.
9. Put them back in the oven for another 15–20 minutes, turning them halfway through cooking on both sides.
10. Take them out of the oven when they are nice and dry and golden brown on both sides.
11. Let them cool in the air covered with a cotton cloth.
12. Freselle can be stored for a long time in paper bags (like bread bags) in a dry, dark place.

TIPS:

Some prefer them crispy and some prefer to run them under water to make them softer; in any case, you can season freselle in a myriad of ways: With a caponata, with a salad of tuna, cherry tomatoes and olives, with grilled vegetables.

Nonna Lucia loved freselle only with fresh cherry tomatoes, olive oil, salt and basil. She said that in her day this was a dish for kings!

In short, whatever you decide to put on it, fresella will always be delicious!

Torta Salata con Zucchine
Savory Pie With Courgettes

Servings: a pan of 8-inch diameter

Ingredients

- 7 oz zucchini
- 8.8 oz flour
- 1.8 oz cornstarch
- 4.2 oz seed oil
- 3 eggs
- 5.3 oz milk
- 1 tsp dry brewer's yeast
- 2 tsp salt
- 1 tsp sugar
- 1.7 oz grated parmesan cheese
- 5.3 oz cooked ham one piece
- 7 oz Emmental one piece

DIRECTIONS:

1. Preheat the oven in fan mode to 360°F.
2. First wash the zucchini and remove the core. Using a large hole grater, grate the zucchini well into a bowl and set it aside.
3. Take the cooked ham and Emmental, cut everything into small cubes and keep aside.
4. Take a bowl and pour in the eggs, parmesan cheese, salt and sugar, mix with a hand whisk.
5. Once everything is mixed well, add the oil in a drizzle and continue to mix vigorously.
6. At this point, add the chopped zucchini to the mixture and continue stirring.
7. Then add the flour, cornstarch and baking powder and mix vigorously.
8. Once the ingredients are blended while stirring pour in the milk in a trickle.
9. Take a wooden spoon or spatula. Pour the ham and Emmental into the mixture and gently mix from top to bottom.
10. Take the baking pan, if you have a bundt pan with a hole in the middle it's even better. Oil it well in each part icon the seed oil and pour it into the mixture.
11. Bake in a hot oven at 360°F for about 40 minutes.
12. Bake and let cool at least 1 hour before serving.

TIPS:

You can substitute prosciutto with salami, bacon or whatever other cold cuts you have in the fridge.
You can make a vegetarian version with peppers, zucchini, and cherry tomatoes. Simply sauté these vegetables in a pan with a little oil and half an onion. Turn off the heat halfway through cooking and add them cold to the mixture instead of the grated courgettes. Continue with the recipe and at the end add just the Emmental.

Taralli Sugna e Pepe
Taralli Sugna e Pepe

Servings: 15 pieces

For the yeast

- 0.3 cup water
- 3.5 oz flour
- 0.28 oz fresh brewer's yeast
  (2.5 g if dehydrated)
- 1 tsp sugar

For the dough of about 15 taralli

- 14 oz flour
- 0.4 cup water
- 7 oz lard
- 5.3 oz almonds
- 4 tsp black pepper
- 0.28 oz fine salt

To decorate

- Almonds to taste

DIRECTIONS:

1. To prepare the taralli sugna e pepe, start with the yeast. In a pitcher with water at room temperature pour and dissolve the yeast with the help of a teaspoon.
2. Then in a bowl pour the flour, sugar and the water and yeast mixture. Knead by hand until you get a batter. Cover the bowl with cling film; leave to rise for at least an hour in a dry place, away from draughts.
3. Grind the almonds until they are not too fine.
4. Move on to the dough: pour the flour into a bowl, add the almond granules, pepper, salt and mix with one hand.
5. Pour in the lard as well and start kneading as you pour in the water.
6. Add the yeast and knead until you have a smooth and homogeneous mixture.
7. Transfer to a pastry board and continue kneading for a few more minutes to mix the ingredients well.
8. Shape taralli. Take 2.5 oz of dough at a time; divide into 2 pieces of 1.2 oz each and make 2 bigoli about 8 inches long. Join the 2 ends and twist the 2 bigoli together until tightly woven. Join the 2 ends together forming a doughnut. Finally, add 4–5 almonds to the surface, pressing lightly so that they barely penetrate the dough and transfer the taralli to a baking tray with a sheet of greaseproof paper.
9. The taralli sugna e pepe bake in a preheated, static oven at 320°F for about 50–60 minutes in the middle rack of the oven; check the cooking time and they will be ready when golden brown.
10. Let them cool completely before enjoying them!

TIPS:

In Naples Taralli Sugna e Pepe are always accompanied by a nice cold beer.
Every summer, in the evening, my grandmother used to take me to the seafront in Naples to get "fresh air" and enjoy the taralli while they were still hot.
This is one of those traditions that I miss from my house and often in the summer, I make my taralli, put them in a paper bag and run to the beach to enjoy them on the beach or on the pier with my nice cold beer. And so I feel a little bit at home.

Alici Marinate
Marinated Anchovies

Servings: 4 people

Ingredients

- 17.5 oz fresh anchovies
- 1 clove of garlic
- 5.3 oz lemon juice
- 0.7 oz parsley
- 5 oz extra virgin olive oil
- Black pepper to taste
- 0.7 oz white wine vinegar
- Salt up to taste

DIRECTIONS:

1. Start with the marinade: in a blender pour the parsley together with a clove of garlic and 1.4 oz of olive oil and mince everything for a few moments.
2. Squeeze the lemons and collect the juice in a bowl along with the olive oil and season with salt and black pepper.
3. Mix well with the help of a hand whisk and, when the 2 mixtures are bound together, add the chopped parsley. Continue to mix with the whisk, then set the marinade aside.
4. Cleaning the anchovies: since the anchovies will not undergo any cooking, I suggest you freeze them for at least 96 hours at -18° (already gutted) and then thaw them and use them in the recipe.
5. Pull off the head, then run your thumb along the belly to open them up, and clean them. Finally rinse the fillets under a trickle of water, being very careful not to split the fish into 2 halves.
6. Place the well-cleaned anchovy fillets in a large tray next to each other and pour the marinade you have prepared, covering the anchovies completely; then cover with cling film. Leave to rest for at least 5 hours at room temperature.
7. After the necessary time has elapsed, remove the foil and pour in the white wine vinegar, stir gently and finally, lightly drain the anchovies from the marinade and arrange them on a serving dish to serve as an appetizer.

TIPS:

This small and inexpensive fish will surprise you in every preparation. Fried or marinated, anchovies are an excellent appetizer to enjoy with friends, especially in summer and with a good glass of white wine!

Zeppole
Soft Seaweed Zeppoline

Servings: 15/20 pieces

Ingredients

- 7 oz flour
- 0.1 oz brewer's yeast
- 1.41 fresh seaweed
- 1 tsp fine salt
- 0.7 cup sparkling water
- Seed oil for frying to taste

DIRECTIONS:

1. Pour the flour into a bowl and gradually add the brewer's yeast dissolved in 0.6 cup of sparkling water. If you don't have sparkling water use plain water or half water and half pale ale.
2. Mix using electric whips so as to avoid lumps. Add the salt. You should obtain an elastic and fluid dough, but not too liquid, so you will have to add more water according to the absorption of the flour.
3. Let rise covered with plastic wrap for about 1 hour until doubled in volume.
4. Add the washed, dried and chopped seaweed.
5. Bring the oil to 350°F in a tall, narrow saucepan.
6. Using one or two spoons, scoop out the batter and put it into the oil, stirring it gently.
7. The seaweed wedges shouldn't turn out very dark, you'll need to pull them out of the oil while they're still pretty light.
8. Place them on paper towels to drain excess oil.
9. Serve them still hot with a pinch of salt.

Pizza Parigina
Parisian Pizza

Servings: 12 pieces

**Ingredients for a
12 x 15-inch baking pan**

- 17.5 oz flour
- 1.3 cup water
- 0.9 oz extra virgin olive oil
- 1 tsp fine salt
- 0.2 oz fresh brewer's yeast
- 0.35 oz sugar

For the stuffing

- 28 oz peeled tomatoes
- 5.3 oz sliced cooked ham
- 10.6 oz caciocavallo or smoked provola cheese

For the surface

- 8 oz puff pastry (1 rectangular roll)
- 2 tbsp fresh liquid cream
- 1 egg yolk

DIRECTIONS:

1. Start with the pizza dough: in a pitcher pour the water at room temperature and dissolve the yeast with the help of a fork.
2. In a bowl pour the flour and sugar and mix by hand before adding the water and yeast a little at a time. Knead by hand, incorporating the water a little at a time until the dough takes on consistency.
3. Pour in the oil, a little at a time. When you have poured half of it add the salt and, after you have incorporated it, add the remaining part of the oil.
4. Knead again until you have a smooth mixture.
5. Now transfer it to the pastry board and continue working for another 10–15 minutes. Press the dough lightly to obtain a smooth and homogeneous ball; if it is too soft you can add a pinch of flour.
6. Then place the ball in a large bowl, cover with foil and let rise at a temperature of 80°F for about 3 hours.
7. In the meantime, drain the peeled tomatoes; remove the skin from the caciocavallo and cut it into thin slices.
8. Once drained, crush the tomatoes with a fork or, if necessary, chop them with a knife.
9. Once risen, the dough should have tripled in volume: remove the foil and pour it into the greased baking dish.
10. Dilate the dough with your fingers, but don't worry if the dough tends to shrink, it's normal: insist without piercing or tearing the dough. Cover the dough again and let it rest for about twenty minutes.
11. After this time, remove the foil and spread the tomato over the entire surface, leaving the edges uncovered.
12. Then cover with the slices of cooked ham. Lay the sliced caciocavallo cheese on top, trying to cover the surface evenly.
13. Finally, roll out the puff pastry, trying to obtain a rectangle large enough to cover the pizza. I advise you to use a ready-made puff pastry because the preparation process would be too long and not at all simple.
14. Place the pastry on the pizza, even out the edges and prick the surface with the prongs of a fork.
15. In a bowl combine and mix egg yolk and cream, then brush the surface with this mixture.
16. Bake in a preheated static oven at 400°F for about 30–35 minutes.
17. Once the cooking time has elapsed, take it out of the oven and leave it to cool for 5 minutes, after which you can remove the pizza Parisienne from the pan and cut it.

TIPS:

This pizza is impossible to find in pizzerias, as the Neapolitan tradition wants it to be a dish with which to have breakfast or a quick snack. So in Naples, you will find it at the bar or in a rotisserie.
I could never find it in America, so my grandmother taught me the recipe so I could make it whenever I wanted. Her motto was: if you can't find it on the street, make it yourself!
I'm sure your guests will love the Parisians at brunch.

Pizzette Rosse
Red Pizzette

Servings: 24 pieces

Ingredients

- 1 cup water at room temperature
- 17.5 oz flour
- 0.3 oz fresh brewer's yeast
- 0.4 oz sugar
- 2 oz extra virgin olive oil
- 0.5 oz fine salt

For the condiment

- 12 oz tomato puree
- 9 oz mozzarella
- 1 tsp fine salt
- Black pepper to taste
- Extra virgin olive oil to taste
- Oregano to taste

DIRECTIONS:

1. Pour the flour into a bowl, along with the crumbled fresh brewer's yeast.
2. Add the room temperature water and stir with a wooden spoon.
3. Add the sugar, salt and pour in the oil as well.
4. Mix again to incorporate the ingredients, then transfer the mixture to a work surface and knead vigorously until smooth.
5. Form a ball with the worked dough, grease a large bowl and transfer the dough inside, cover with cling film and leave to rise for about 3 hours at room temperature, away from draughts or in a switched-off oven with the light on. At the end of the rising time, the dough will have tripled in volume.
6. In a bowl pour the tomato, season with salt, pepper, oregano and oil. Mix everything with a spoon and set aside until you need to use it.
7. Transfer the risen dough onto a pastry board and sprinkle with very little flour; roll out with a rolling pin until you have a rectangle about 0.15 inches thick.
8. Cup the dough with a 3-inch diameter ramekin or the wet edge of a glass cup.
9. Take the excess dough, shape it into a ball and let it rest covered for about 10 minutes. You can knead the excess dough again and make more pizzettas.
10. Place the pizzas on the greased baking sheet. Once arranged, form a little pocket in the center, leaving about a 0.2-inch border.
11. Dice the mozzarella and dress the center of the pizzette with the tomato and diced mozzarella; add a drizzle of oil and a pinch of oregano to taste.
12. Bake the pizzettas in a static oven preheated to 400°F for 15 minutes: For the first 10 minutes place the pan at the base of the oven; the remaining 5 minutes on the highest rack.
13. Once cooked, pop the red pizzas in the oven and serve them hot!

TIPS:

This is a quick and easy recipe, ideal for a birthday party or brunch. The pizzette can be topped as you prefer, for example with vegetables and mozzarella, or with a cream of pumpkin, crumbled sausage and mozzarella. In short, have fun creating many variations to your liking.

Grissini al Formaggio
Grana Padano Breadsticks

Servings: 20 pieces

Ingredients

- 9 oz flour
- ½ cup lukewarm water
- 2 oz Grana Padano DOP to grate
- 0.7 oz extra virgin olive oil
- ½ tsp fresh brewer's yeast
- 0.2 oz fine salt
- Sesame seeds to taste
- Pumpkin seeds to taste
- Linseed to taste

DIRECTIONS:

1. Dissolve the yeast in the water, stirring with a spoon.
2. Pour the flour and the grated Grana Padano DOP into a bowl and add salt.
3. Pour in the water in which you dissolved the yeast and incorporate the olive oil. Mix with your hands to mix the ingredients and absorb the liquids.
4. Once you have a homogeneous mixture, transfer it to a pastry board and knead it again to create a compact dough.
5. Transfer to a bowl, cover with cling film and leave to rise for 1 hour in the oven with the light switched off or in a warm place. After this time your dough will have risen.
6. Dust a pastry board with flour, roll out the dough with a rolling pin to a thickness of about 0.1 inches.
7. Using a smooth pastry cutter, cut out strips about 0.8 inches wide. Roll the strips on the pastry board with your hands to form the classic breadsticks and place them on a baking tray lined with greaseproof paper.
8. Brush the surface of the breadsticks with water.
9. Scatter seeds as desired and bake in a static oven preheated to 375°F for 18 minutes.
10. When cooked, take the Grana Padano breadsticks out of the oven and let them cool before eating.

TIPS:

Usually when I make Grissini, I always make two variations of them; this one I just described and one that I'm going to brush with a little garlic butter instead.
This recipe is a must during my brunches with friends because it's quick and versatile.

Cips di Patate al Pepe e Limone
Potato Chips With Pink Pepper and Lemon

Servings: 4 people

Ingredients

- 6 potatoes (medium size)
- Peanut seed oil to taste
- Salt to taste
- Pink pepper to taste
- 1 lemon

DIRECTIONS:

1. Peel the potatoes and cut them into thin slices. Put them in a bowl with plenty of cold water and salt.
2. Pour the peanut oil into a high-sided skillet and bring it to 350°F.
3. Dry the potatoes well before frying and dip them in the oil until golden brown.
4. A piece of advice: when frying, to eliminate excess oil, do not immediately put down what you have just fried on blotting paper. This will have the opposite effect, the food will absorb the oil and will not be crispy. On the contrary, take what you have just fried out of the pan with the help of a skimmer or, even better, with kitchen tongs. Drain off the excess oil for about 30 seconds, keeping it on the frying pan so that it retains its heat. Then place the fried fish on absorbent paper.
5. Press a lemon, extract the juice by removing the seeds.
6. When you have fried all the potatoes put them in a bowl and let them cool for about 20 minutes.
7. After this time, pour the lemon juice over the potatoes a little at a time, stirring continuously.
8. Sprinkle with plenty of pink pepper and salt to taste and toss them in the bowl.
9. The potato chips with pepper and lemon are ready.

TIPS:

Serve them hot and of course, if you don't like pepper, you can omit it or replace it with paprika or even garlic powder. Accompany the potatoes with the sauce of your choice!

Focaccia Pugliese
Apulian Focaccia

Servings: 6 people

Ingredients

- 8.8 oz flour
- 8.8 oz refined semolina flour
- 1.5 cup warm water
- 0.4 oz fresh brewer's yeast
  (or 4 g dry brewer's yeast)
- 1 medium potato
- 0.2 oz salt
- 1 tsp honey
- Cherry tomatoes to taste
- Oregano to taste
- Extra virgin olive oil to taste

DIRECTIONS:

1. Boil the potato, remove the skin and puree it with a potato masher. Let cool.
2. Dissolve dry or fresh brewer's yeast in about 0.2 cup of water. Mix well.
3. In a bowl sift the flour, then add the mashed potatoes, the dissolved yeast, honey and mix the ingredients adding the remaining water.
4. Now add the salt and continue to knead vigorously in the bowl or on the work surface to obtain a smooth, well-blended and very sticky mixture.
5. Cover the bowl with plastic wrap and let rise in a warm place for about 2–3 hours. The dough should double in volume.
6. After the time is up, turn the oven to 425°F.
7. Grease the pan with oil and brush it all over the surface, including the edges.
8. Pour the risen dough into the pan and with oiled fingertips spread it out.
9. Season with washed cherry tomatoes divided in half that you will put on the surface pressing them lightly to make them adhere to the dough, add a drizzle of oil and oregano.
10. Bake the focaccia Pugliese in a preheated oven for about 20 minutes.
11. For the last 5 minutes move the pan to high and set the oven to grill mode to get a nice browning.
12. Let cool and cut into squares or slices.

TIPS:

You can also dress the focaccia with just oil and rosemary, or with black olives and thyme. Try it in various variations and choose your favorite.

Rustici Leccesi
Rustici Leccesi

Servings: 8 pieces

Ingredients

- 32 oz puff pastry (about 4 rolls)
- 1 oz tomato puree
- 1.3 oz mozzarella
- Extra virgin olive oil to taste
- Salt up to taste

For the béchamel

- 7 oz whole milk
- 0.7 oz flour
- 0.7 oz butter
- Salt up to taste
- Black pepper to taste
- Nutmeg to taste

For brushing

- 1 egg

DIRECTIONS:

1. First, prepare the béchamel sauce: heat the milk in a saucepan and, separately, melt the butter in a saucepan over low heat; add the flour and stir quickly with a whisk to prevent lumps from forming. When the flour is completely blended, add the hot milk and let everything thicken over moderate heat, stirring constantly. Season with nutmeg, salt and pepper, then cover the béchamel with plastic wrap.
2. Cut the mozzarella into slices and then chop finely; if it is too wet, leave it to dry in a colander.
3. Season the tomato puree with a little oil and salt.
4. Cut out 16 circles from the puff pastry rolls with a 4-inch diameter pastry cutter and 8 circles with a 3-inch diameter pastry cutter.
5. Place 8 large circles on a baking tray covered with greaseproof paper, brush the surface with the beaten egg and place another circle of the same size on top. This will help the pastry to puff up and make it puff.
6. Put 1 tsp of béchamel sauce in the center of the disc, then a tsp of tomato puree and some chopped mozzarella.
7. Brush the edges with egg and cover the large discs with the smaller ones, sealing the edges well.
8. Proceed like this with all the discs and at the end brush the rustici with more beaten egg.
9. Bake them in a static oven preheated to 400°F for about 20 minutes, until golden brown.
10. Once ready, pop them in the oven and let them cool before serving!

Moussaka
Greek Moussaka

Servings: 4 people

Ingredients

- 53 oz eggplants
- 17.5 oz potatoes
- 17.5 oz ground lamb
- 17.5 oz ground pork
- 2 medium onions
- 2 cloves of garlic
- 5 tbsp extra virgin olive oil
- Salt up to taste
- Black pepper to taste
- ½ tsp cinnamon powder
- 0.3 cup of red wine
- 17.5 oz copper tomatoes
- 5.3 oz pecorino cheese to grate
- 3.5 oz parmesan cheese pdo to grate

For the béchamel

- 4 cups milk
- 3.5 oz butter
- 3.5 oz flour
- Nutmeg to taste
- Salt up to taste

For frying

- Peanut oil

DIRECTIONS:

1. Wash the eggplants and remove the green part on the end, then dry them and cut them into slices.
2. Put the eggplants, one slice on top of the other, in a colander sprinkling them with coarse salt and add a weight that can crush them. Wait a couple of hours and let drain all the liquids.
3. In a large frying pan, put the oil, add the chopped onions and crushed garlic, then leave to brown and then add the minced lamb and pork.
4. Sauté over high heat stirring well until the meat is well browned, then add the red wine and let the alcohol evaporate completely, add salt, pepper and a pinch of cinnamon. Leave to cook over gentle heat and then add the skinned and diced copper tomatoes; mix well, put a lid on the pan and leave to cook over low heat for about 1 hour, stirring occasionally. The sauce should dry slowly.
5. In the meantime peel the potatoes, cut them into thin slices and boil them for 5 minutes in salted water, then remove them from the water and put them to drain, placing them delicately in a colander.
6. Rinse the eggplants under running water and then dry them. Fry them and remove excess oil by placing them on a plate lined with paper towels.
7. In the same way, fry the potatoes and drain them of excess oil.
8. Now prepare the béchamel sauce with the ingredients written above and follow the recipe that you will have memorized by now. (Neapolitan pasta frittatine recipe)
9. Now move on to the assembly. Take a 10 x 12 inch sized baking pan and line its bottom by sprinkling it with the potatoes.
10. On top put half of the fried eggplant, then half of the meat sauce and finally sprinkle with 2–3 tbsp of grated cheese mixed together.
11. Repeat the layers (without potatoes) and then pour half of the leftover cheese into the béchamel, mixing well. Pour all the béchamel sauce over the preparation, sprinkle with the remaining cheese and bake in a preheated oven at 360°F for about 40–45 minutes.
12. As soon as the béchamel becomes golden brown, remove the pan and let the moussaka cool and compact.
13. Cut the moussaka into squares, plate it and serve immediately. Kalí órexi, enjoy!

Verdure in Pastella
Fried Mixed Vegetables

Servings: 4 people

For the batter

- 9 oz flour
- ½ cup sparkling water (very cold)
- 1 tsp instant yeast for savory preparations

For the vegetables

- 1 eggplant
- 1 zucchini
- 1 pepper
- Peanut oil to taste
- Salt to taste

DIRECTIONS:

1. First clean and chop the vegetables for frying. Wash the bell pepper, eggplant and zucchini well.
2. Cut the zucchini and eggplant into rounds and the bell pepper into strips.
3. Place the vegetables on a sheet of kitchen paper to make them as dry as possible.
4. In a glass bowl pour the sifted flour and sifted instant yeast. Add the very cold sparkling water a little at a time and mix vigorously with a whisk to obtain a smooth and homogeneous mixture.
5. In a narrow, high-sided pan, pour peanut oil and bring to 350°F.
6. Dip the vegetables into the batter. Start with the zucchini, then put them in the batter and with a fork move them to the frying oil. Fry a few pieces at a time so as not to lower the temperature of the oil.
7. Using a skimmer, drain the vegetables and place them on a sheet of kitchen paper.
8. Do the same thing with the peppers and eggplant.
9. Once all the battered vegetables are ready, put the mixed fried vegetables on a plate, salt and enjoy them hot.

TIPS:

To make battered vegetables you can use the vegetables you prefer or those in season.
You can also fry fish such as prawns with this type of batter.
I recommend that you don't salt the batter, fried foods should always be salted afterwards, otherwise they lose their crunchiness and, above all, always use peanut oil for frying because it keeps the high temperatures.

Pizza Fritta
Neapolitan Fried Pizza

Servings: 4 pieces

Ingredients

- 17.5 oz Manitoba flour
- 1.3 cup water
- 0.1 oz dry brewer's yeast
- 0.3 oz fine salt

For the stuffing

- 10 oz ricotta di bufala
- 3.5 oz provolone cheese
- 7 oz peeled tomatoes
- 2 oz salami Napoli type
- 8 leaves basil
- Salt up to taste
- Black pepper to taste

For frying

- 5 cups seed oil

DIRECTIONS:

1. To make the fried pizza, pour the sifted flour and dry brewer's yeast into a planetary mixer (fitted with a dough hook). Add 1.3 cups of water and run the mixer.
2. Continue to add water a little at a time while the planetary mixer is in action, taking care to wait until the liquid is well absorbed before adding more. Once you've poured ¾ of the total amount of water, add the salt, continuing to knead.
3. Add the remainder of the water and leave it to work until you have a smooth and homogeneous mixture.
4. Take the dough out of the mixer and move it to a lightly floured surface. Roll it out lightly with your hands then fold the edges towards the center. Then fold the dough into itself to give it a spherical shape. Transfer the dough into a large bowl, cover with cling film and leave to rise in the oven with the light switched off, until it has tripled in volume. It will take about 3 hours.
5. After this time, recover the dough and transfer it to a lightly floured pastry board. Form a loaf, then divide it into 4 equal parts and knead each piece into small balls.
6. Transfer the balls of dough on a tray well apart from each other, cover them with cling film (otherwise the dough will not develop) and leave to rise for another 3 hours in the oven with the light off.
7. In the meantime prepare the filling: cut the salami and provolone into small cubes.
8. Prepare the basil leaves and the ricotta cheese: work it for a few moments with a spoon in a bowl to make it creamier.
9. After the 3 hours of rising, take the balls of dough and roll them out with your hands on a lightly floured pastry board, you must create an irregular disc of about 12 inches in diameter.
10. Now you can deal with the filling, you have to use 1/4 of the doses of the ingredients for each pizza, filling only one half of the disk and leaving clean a couple of centimeters from the edge.
11. Spread out a layer of ricotta then lightly mash the peeled tomatoes with a fork and pour them over the ricotta salting to taste, then add a few cubes of salami and provolone. Perfume with fresh basil leaves chopped by hand.
12. Fold over the unfilled half of the disc to create a half-moon shape. Seal the edges well to prevent the filling from leaking out during cooking.
13. Once you have made all 4 pizzas you can take care of the cooking: Heat the oil in a pan to 350°F. Dip one pizza at a time, while it's cooking wet it with a spoon with the hot oil to coat it well; be sure to gently turn it on its other side to cook it evenly and continue frying until the pizza is a nice golden color.
14. Drain the pizza with a slotted spoon, place it on paper towels to dry the excess oil.
15. The fried pizza is ready to be enjoyed piping hot!

TIPS:

The fried pizza is a delight to enjoy accompanied. You can fill it as you prefer; the classic Neapolitan recipe calls for a filling of Cicoli (or ciccioli), Ricotta, Provola, Salt and plenty of Pepper.
Have fun finding your favorite filling or prepare 4 different fillings so you can taste 4 variations!

Panzarotti Pugliesi Fritti
Pugliese Fried Panzerotti

Servings: 15 pieces

Ingredients

- 10 oz ground semolina flour
- 9 oz flour
- 0.6 cup warm water
- 0.6 cup milk
- 0,4 oz salt
- 2 tsp sugar
- 3 tbsp extra virgin olive oil
- 0.3 oz fresh brewer's yeast

For the stuffing

- 6 tbsp tomato sauce (or peeled tomatoes)
- 35 oz mozzarella
- 4 tbsp canestrato pugliese or parmesan cheese
- 5 leaves basil
- Salt to taste
- 4 cups peanut seed oil

DIRECTIONS:

1. In a planetary mixer put the lukewarm water, milk at room temperature, sugar, oil and yeast. Run the mixer until the yeast is well dissolved.
2. Now gradually add the flour and salt. Let the planetary mixer work for about 10 minutes, then take the dough ball and transfer it to a lightly floured pastry board and continue to knead it well until you get a smooth and homogeneous dough.
3. Put the covered loaf to rise in the oven off with the light on for about 2 hours.
4. In the meantime, cut the mozzarella into small cubes and pour it into a colander with a plate underneath. Pour in also the tomato sauce and a little salt and turn well. Put in the fridge and give the mozzarella and tomato time to lose their water.
5. After 2 hours of rising take the dough and form many balls that will grow for another 1 hour always covered in the oven with the light off.
6. After 1 hour, roll out each ball with a rolling pin.
7. Take the filling and add the basil leaves chopped by hand and the grated cheese. Mix everything together well.
8. Pour the filling into each panzerotti with a spoon, leaving one half and the edges clean.
9. Firmly close the panzerotti creating a half moon, seal the edges well and also help yourself with the end of a fork to prevent the panzerotti from opening during cooking.
10. Immediately fry them no more than three at a time and turn them occasionally to cook them evenly.
11. Once golden brown, drain them with a slotted spoon, place them on a sheet of paper towels and serve the panzerotti still hot.

TIPS:

As with all traditional Mediterranean stuffed delicacies, you can have fun creating the filling you prefer; I, for example, love the fried panzerotti stuffed with ricotta and spinach that grandma Lucia used to make. The only thing you must always pay attention to is to have a dry and not liquid filling, so whatever food you choose to put inside the panzerotti, let it drain well.

Panzanella
Panzanella

Servings: 4 people

Ingredients

- 12 oz stale Tuscan bread (or classic oven bread)
- 8 oz ripe ramato tomatoes
- 7 oz cucumbers
- 3.2 oz red onions
- Basil to taste
- 1 cup water (varies depending on how wet the bread needs to be)
- 2 oz white wine vinegar
- Extra virgin olive oil to taste
- Salt up to taste
- Black pepper to taste

DIRECTIONS:

1. Cut the bread into coarse cubes. Put it in a bowl and add the water and vinegar.
2. Mix it up so the bread can absorb the wetness evenly and keep it aside.
3. Cut the tomatoes first into quarters and then into smaller pieces.
4. Peel the skin off the cucumber, trim off the ends and split it in half lengthwise, then slice it thinly.
5. Finally, peel the onion, cut it in half and slice it thinly.
6. Pick up the bowl with the bread and mix again, then add the onions and cucumbers.
7. Add the tomatoes and mix everything together and add the basil.
8. Add the salt, pepper, and oil (maximum 3 tbsp). Mix again and refrigerate the Panzanella until ready to serve!

TIPS:

There are many variations of Panzanella. Customize it with the vegetables you prefer. For example, I add black olives and crumbled feta to the traditional recipe. This dish, although very simple, will be delicious for your guests.

Vitello Tonnato
Tonned Calf

Servings: 6 people

Ingredients

- 28 oz calf
- 1 stalk celery
- 1 carrot
- 1 golden onion
- 1 clove of garlic
- 1 cup white wine
- 0.4 gal water
- 1 bay leaf
- 3 cloves
- 3 tbsp extra virgin olive oil
- ½ tsp black peppercorns
- 2 pinches fine salt

For the sauce

- 2 eggs
- 3.5 oz tuna in oil, drained
- 3 fillets anchovies in oil
- 0,2 oz capers in salt
- Caper berries to decorate to taste

DIRECTIONS:

1. Wash the vegetables, peel and trim the carrot, and cut it into pieces. Remove the ends from the celery and cut it into pieces. Peel the onion and divide it into 2 parts. Gradually collect the ingredients in a bowl and add the whole peeled garlic.
2. Clean the meat by removing any gristle and fatty filaments.
3. In a large pot put the piece of veal, the roughly chopped vegetables, the bay leaf, 2–3 cloves and the black peppercorns.
4. Pour in the white wine and then the water, which should cover everything. Add 2 pinches of salt and then the oil.
5. Turn on the stove and wait until it comes to a boil, then gradually remove the foam that will rise to the surface.
6. Close the lid and lower the heat slightly, letting it cook for about 40–45 minutes. The meat (in the center) mustn't exceed 149°F.
7. Once the meat is cooked, remove it and let it cool completely.
8. Remove bay leaves, pepper and cloves from broth and meat.
9. Recover 1/3 of the obtained broth and let it reduce on a high flame for about 10 minutes. At the end of cooking drain the vegetables in a bowl.
10. Immerse the fresh eggs in a saucepan with plenty of cold water. Turn on the stove and count 9 minutes from the moment of boiling. When they are hard, drain them and rinse under cold water. Once cool, shell them and cut them into 4 parts.
11. Add the egg wedges to the bowl with the vegetables.
12. Add the drained tuna, anchovies in oil and capers (rinse under running water first).
13. Add a little broth. Blend everything with the immersion blender and add more broth as needed. Blend until smooth.
14. At this point, the meat should be completely cold. Cut it into thin slices with a smooth-bladed knife.
15. Arrange the slices on a serving dish and pour the cream in the middle. Finally decorate with capers, some whole and some cut in half, and your Vitello tonnato with the traditional Piedmontese recipe is ready!

TIPS:

Veal Tonnato is a Piedmontese dish that in the past could not miss on the tables of noble families, as an appetizer or aperitif. Today the recipe for the accompanying cream has undergone some variations, some people use mayonnaise instead of eggs. You can keep the veal in the fridge for a maximum of 2–3 days, covered with plastic wrap and not together with the sauce.

Anelli di Cipolla di Tropea Fritti
Frittelle of Tropea Onions

Servings: 10 pieces

Ingredients

- 21 oz red onions from Tropea
- 2 tbsp fine salt
- 3.5 oz flour 00
- 50 g water
- Parsley to taste
- Sunflower oil for frying to taste

DIRECTIONS:

1. Peel the onions and cut them into thin slices.
2. Transfer them to a colander that you have placed over a bowl and sprinkle with 2 tbsp of salt.
3. Mix well with your hands, massaging them for about 10 minutes, until they have softened and released the liquid.
4. Rinse them to remove excess salt, drain from water and transfer to a bowl.
5. Chop the parsley and add it to the onions.
6. Add the flour, mix it all together and add the water as well.
7. Work the mixture with your hands until completely blended and adjust the salt.
8. Heat plenty of oil until it reaches a temperature of 350°F, then using 2 spoons, create pancakes and dip them in the oil, a few at a time.
9. Cook them for about 8 minutes, until they are well browned, then drain them on a tray lined with kitchen paper, to remove excess oil and serve the Tropea onion fritters still hot.

Meal Plan

	BREAKFAST	LUNCH	DINNER
DAY 1	Milk, Wholemeal Bread with Jam.	Pasta and Beans.	Meatballs with Sauce.
DAY 2	Greek Yogurt and Almonds.	Pumpkin Risotto.	Piadina Romagnola.
DAY 3	Zucchini Omelette.	Spaghetti with Fresh Tomatoes.	Potato Gateau.
DAY 4	Milk, Whole Grain Cereal.	Tagliatelle Boscaiola Style.	Scarpone Aubergines.
DAY 5	Tea with Cantucci.	Orecchiette with Turnip Tops.	Onion Omelette
DAY 6	Greek Pita with Spreadable Cheese.	Pasta and Potatoes.	Mozzarella in a Wagon.
DAY 7	Milk, Seasonal Fruit.	Lasagna.	Baked King Prawns.
DAY 8	Milk, Wholemeal Bread, Jam.	Pasta and Pesto alla Genovese.	Milanese Schnitzel.
DAY 9	Asparagus Omelette.	Risotto with Pescatora.	Peperonata
DAY 10	Tea with Lady Kisses.	Tortellini in Broth.	Chicken Cacciatora.
DAY 11	Greek Yogurt and Hazelnuts.	Spaghetti Amatriciana.	Mushroom Eggplants.
DAY 12	Milk, Whole Grain Cereal.	Saffron Risotto.	Escalope with Lemon.
DAY 13	Tea, Seasonal Fruit.	Spaghetti Puttanesca.	Codfish Stew with Polenta.
DAY 14	Greek Pita with Tomatoes and Salad.	Neapolitan Ragout.	Parmigiana of Potatoes.
DAY 15	Milk, Wholemeal Bread, Jam.	Spaghetti with Garlic, Oil and Chili Peppers.	Marinated Salmon.

	BREAKFAST	LUNCH	DINNER
DAY 16	Milk, Wholemeal Bread with Jam.	Spaghetti with Clams.	Fried Meatballs.
DAY 17	Greek Yogurt and Almonds.	Neapolitan Rice Timbale.	Fried Calamari.
DAY 18	Zucchini Omelette.	Spaghetti Nerano Style.	Peppers Stuffed with Meat.
DAY 19	Milk, Whole Grain Cereal.	Fish Soup.	Bream in Acqua Pazza.
DAY 20	Tea with Cantucci.	Spaghetti Carbonara.	Baked Kid with Potatoes.
DAY 21	Greek Pita with Spreadable Cheese.	Gnocchi alla Sorrentina.	Neapolitan Mountaineers.
DAY 22	Milk, Seasonal Fruit.	Baked Cannelloni.	Green Chillies with Tomato.
DAY 23	Milk, Wholemeal Bread, Jam.	Baked Pasta.	Roastbeef Neapolitan Style.
DAY 24	Asparagus Omelette.	Risotto with Pescatora.	Freselle Napoletane with Oil and Tomatoes.
DAY 25	Tea with Lady Kisses.	Tortellini in Broth.	Savory Pie with Courgettes.
DAY 26	Greek Yogurt and Hazelnuts.	Pasta alla Gricia	Marinated Anchovies.
DAY 27	Milk, Whole Grain Cereal.	Bolognese Ragout.	Apulian Focaccia.
DAY 28	Tea, Seasonal Fruit.	Fettuccine Alfredo.	Greek Moussaka.
DAY 29	Greek Pita with Tomatoes and Salad.	Ravioli with Ricotta and Spinach.	Panzanella.
DAY 30	Milk, Wholemeal Bread, Jam.	Spaghetti with Garlic, Oil and Chili Peppers.	Tonned Calf.

Printed in Great Britain
by Amazon

11222184R00079